Agile Software Development with C# and Visual Studio 2022
Third Edition

Lynn Smith

DEDICATION

To All Readers of This Book.

CONTENTS

Preface

This book, designed for beginners, will introduce you to the field of agile software development with C#. There are many books on C# and just as many, if not more, on agile, but few teach a programming language and software development methodology in conjunction.

Agile blurs the lines between the roles of analyst, designer, programmer, and tester. Therefore, when you learn agile, you will learn to analyze, design, develop, and test. By combining C# and agile in one book, you will be able to experience all roles through a single journey. At the end of the book, you will be given several tiny C# projects to work on following agile philosophy. Working through these projects with four or five other readers (e.g., as in a college setting) would further benefit your understanding.

This book is not a reference, so content will be kept at a minimum. This book is also not an in-depth cover of any specific topic, instead designed to cater to beginners. Readers may always research the web for further details.

This book requires you to type all code. We don't provide sample code downloads. Though we understand your time is valuable, we believe hands-on practice is the best way to learn.

Throughout the book, you will be given plenty of exercises under the titles of **Programming Challenge** and **Test Your Understanding**. We strongly encourage you to try all exercises as you work through the book.

This third edition uses Visual Studio 2022 Community as the development environment.

Last but not least, we thank Dr. Youlong Zhuang for reviewing this third edition and providing valuable suggestions.

Chapter 1: Introduction to C# and Agile

Chapter Learning Outcomes

1.1 Recognizing C# as an object-oriented programming language

1.2 Generating a simple program with C# and Visual Studio

1.3 Recalling phases in traditional waterfall software development approach

1.4 Recalling values in Agile Manifesto

1.5 Recognizing the differences between waterfall and agile

1.1 What is C#?

C# is an object-oriented programming (OOP) language for developing application software. An application consists of instructions for the computer, and C# is the language that programmers use to write those instructions. In this book, you will learn how to follow C# syntax to form the instructions.

As a modern programming language, C# is often considered easier to learn, yet more powerful than other programming languages, such as C, C++, or Java.

An object-oriented programming language is a way to develop applications with reusable classes that can be used to build larger programs. A class is a container with a collection of instructions in it. A class can be used in multiple places of a program or even in another program without having to rewrite the instructions. To use instructions in a class, you create an object of that class. Then all instructions of that class are available with the object.

Before you can start to code in C#, you need to install Visual Studio 2022 Community edition. Search the web for "download visual studio 2022 community edition" and click on the "free download" link to download the software. After downloading the file to your local computer, double click to install it.

On the "Visual Studio Installer" window, make sure you check ".NET desktop development" before clicking on the "install" button.

What you have just installed is an Integrated Development Environment (IDE), which includes a text editor to type code into and a debugger to test your code.

After installation is complete, follow the instructions to restart the computer and you are on your way to becoming a C# programmer. Make sure you close all other programs before restarting to avoid losing any unsaved work.

Test Your Understanding 1.1
C# is an OOP _____ that programmers use to write _____ for computers.
A. language, instructions
B. language, manual
C. editor, instructions
D. editor, manual

Test Your Understanding 1.2
An object-oriented programming language is a way to develop applications such that _____ classes can be used to build larger programs.
A. any
B. useless
C. reusable
D. small

Test Your Understanding 1.3
What is included in Visual Studio IDE?
A. A text editor for typing in code
B. A text editor for typing in code and turning in homework
C. A text editor for typing in code and a debugger to test the code
D. A visually appealing text editor liked by many programmers

1.2 Your First C# Program

On your PC's desktop, create a new folder named 'Agile'. You will save all project files in this folder for organization purposes.

Launch Visual Studio. The first time you start Visual Studio, it will prompt if you want to sign in by creating an account. I suggest that you create an account now even though it has the option, "Not now, maybe later". If you don't create an account, it will prompt you again after 30 days without the 'not now' option. Creating an account only requires an email address.

Start a new project by clicking "Create a new project" on the launch page (Figure 1.1).

Get started

 Clone or check out code
Get code from an online repository like GitHub or Azure DevOps

 Open a project or solution
Open a local Visual Studio project or .sln file

Open a local folder
Navigate and edit code within any folder

 Create a new project
Choose a project template with code scaffolding to get started

Continue without code →

Figure 1.1 Launch page of Visual Studio 2022 Community edition.

In the "Create a new project" window, type "C# console app core" into the "Search for project templates" search box. Select the option that includes C# and .NET Core (top one in Figure 1.2). Click "Next".

Figure 1.2 Create a new project window.

A new window, "Configure your new project", will pop up. Give a name to the project, e.g. Chapter1Example1. Browse for the location you want to save the project to by clicking on the "…" symbol on the right. Check the "Place solution and project in the same location" box (Figure 1.3). Click the "Next" button to continue.

— □ ×

Configure your new project

Console App   C#   Linux   macOS   Windows   Console

Project name

Chapter1Example1

Location

C:\Users\smith\Desktop\Agile

Solution name ⓘ

Chapter1Example1

☑ Place solution and project in the same directory

Back   Next

Figure 1.3 Configure your new project.

— □ ×

Additional information

Console App   C#   Linux   macOS   Windows   Console

Framework ⓘ

.NET 6.0 (Long-term support)

Back   Create

Figure 1.4 Select .NET 6.0 for additional information.

Finally, click on the "Create" button to create the project.

This may take a few minutes the first time. A default program with default code will be displayed as shown in Figure 1.5. If you don't see the default program, check the "Solution Explorer" window on the right side to see if "Program.cs" is selected (double clicking on this file name will display the code in the code window). The "Solution Explorer" window is shown in Figure 1.6.

Program.cs ⊣ ✕

C# Chapter1Example1

```
1    // See https://aka.ms/new-console-template for more information
2    Console.WriteLine("Hello, World!");
3
```

Figure 1.5 Default code window.

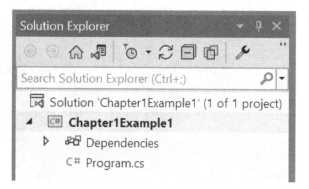

Figure 1.6 Solution Explorer window

Delete all lines of code in Figure 1.5. Add one line of instruction as shown in Figure 1.7.

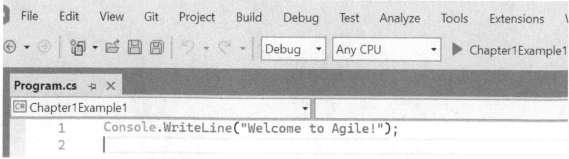

Figure 1.7 Your first C# program.

Finally, click on the little green triangle "Play" button (Chapter1Example1) on the top (Figure 1.7) to run the program. The result is shown in Figure 1.8.

CSS Microsoft Visual Studio Debug Console

Welcome to Agile!

Figure 1.8 A console window with the program running.

You have just used Visual Studio IDE to write your first application in C# and to run the program. You can now push the enter key to close the program.

1.3 Explanation for Your First Program

Refer to Figure 1.7, "Your First C# program", for this explanation.

There is only one line of code for the computer to follow. The instruction tells the computer to display the text "Welcome to Agile!" on the console screen. It uses a pre-developed class called Console. The Console class has a method called WriteLine() that will display the message on the console. "Welcome to Agile" is a C# string literal and must be inside a pair of quotation marks.

A class in C# is a container that often has many methods in it. A method is a group of instructions for a common objective. The Console class has many methods. In the code window, after type the class name "Console" and a dot, you see a popup menu for all available methods and properties.

Figure 1.9 Methods, properties, and events of Console class.

You just created a program with C# by writing one line of code and using premade classes (Console) and methods (WriteLine())!

Test Your Understanding 1.4
A class is a container that groups things, such as _____, together.
A. methods
B. namespaces
C. instructions
D. statements

Test Your Understanding 1.5
A(n) _____ is a logical group of C# statements for a common objective.
A. namespace
B. class
C. method
D. instruction

Test Your Understanding 1.6
In the following statement, what is "Console"?
Console.WriteLine("Welcome to Agile!");
A. a namespace
B. a class
C. a method
D. a computer monitor

Test Your Understanding 1.7
In the following statement, what is "WriteLine"?
Console.WriteLine("Welcome to Agile!");
A. a namespace
B. a class
C. a method
D. a computer monitor

Programming Challenge 1.1

Chapter1Example1 has one line of instruction (Figure 1.7). You can add more. Pay attention to the sequence of the instructions and how they affect the result. Add a line of code to the program in Figure 1.7 so that, when the program runs, the console will make a beep sound.

Add another line of code to the program so that, when the program runs, the background color of the console will change to green. Is the whole console screen green?

After the green background color instruction, add a statement to display "Welcome again!".

Insert a line of code as the first line to the program so that, when the program runs, all the text in the console is red. Are all texts red?

Use the Task class to pause the console for 3 seconds.

Finally, use the Clear method of the Console class to erase all text on the console.

1.4 What Is Software Development?

There are several philosophies on software development. We will examine two major approaches. Let's use an example to explain the concepts.

Mr. Lincoln has been the owner of a small toy retailer since 1994. He worked in toy manufacturing for many years before being laid off when the company moved the whole manufacturing operation to China. He decided to use his experience with the toy industry and became a retailer that sold toys made in China. He was told that computers can increase his business's efficiency and effectiveness. One difficulty he has with his business is keeping track of inventory and the price of each product. He decided to buy a laptop and recently started using it. After a few days using the laptop, though, he decided that computers saved paper, but made little difference otherwise. Can you develop an efficient application to help Mr. Lincoln?

Mr. Lincoln's computer needs application software that can help him keep track of inventory and prices.

A small group of students from a local university taking a systems analysis and design course volunteered to help Mr. Lincoln.

They start by interviewing Mr. Lincoln about his business mission and strategy, business operations, budget, timeline, and scope for the software development. Following the Systems Development Life Cycle (SDLC) from their textbook, they are beginning the planning phase. In a couple of days, they turn in a business plan which includes all they can find out about the business and a feasibility study on the project. The students plan to develop an application with C# to handle the inventory with little cost to Mr. Lincoln.

The professor of the class and Mr. Lincoln approve the business plan based on the benefits and costs of the project, the manageable scope, and the timeline. The group then starts the analysis phase: determining the software requirements from Mr. Lincoln.

Mr. Lincoln wants something simple and easy to use. He wants to be able to update or enter new inventory whenever a new shipment from a supplier arrives. The application needs to be able to automatically update the inventory whenever a sale is made. He also wants to have the ability to quickly check the price for a certain toy. Finally, Mr. Lincoln wants to be able to have a print of his inventory on paper and a print of the receipt for customers. During the interview, the students ask many questions, such as the product return policy, issues regarding inventory loss from theft or damage in transit, and data about suppliers, products, and sales. They also want to know if Mr. Lincoln keeps a price update history. The students then write the analysis report outlining the detailed requirements from Mr. Lincoln and submit copies to the professor and Mr. Lincoln. This is the analysis phase of SDLC.

After the professor and Mr. Lincoln approve the requirements, the group begins the design phase. They draw a case diagram to show the interaction between the users and the system. It clearly defines what features the system will have and the boundary of the system. They have mock up screens for Mr. Lincoln to see if that is the user interface he wants. The specifications for all input and output forms are completed. Entity Relationship Diagrams for the business data are reviewed by the professor.

After the professor and Mr. Lincoln approve the design, the team starts to actually code. They use C# and make sure all code runs as expected. They also ask Mr. Lincoln to complete a user acceptance test to make sure he really likes the application. This is called the development phase of SDLC.

Both the team and Mr. Lincoln fully test the system and feel it is a good replacement for Mr. Lincoln's spreadsheet-based system. The team then publishes the application in Mr. Lincoln's working computer. The team also leaves a simple user manual, just in case Mr. Lincoln gets lost while using the new system. This is called the deploy phase of SDLC.

A few days later, the team meets with Mr. Lincoln and asks about his experience with the new system. Mr. Lincoln made a long list of things he wants to change. The team politely says they will discuss it with the professor and come back to Mr. Lincoln. Unfortunately, it's close to the end of the semester, and nobody wants to continue with Mr. Lincoln's change request, since the whole application may need to start all over again. They wish Mr. Lincoln told them earlier. This stage is often called maintenance, which can lead to a new round of SDLC.

Test Your Understanding 1.8
With SDLC, a feasibility study of the project is typically included in the _____ phase.
A. planning
B. analysis
C. design
D. development

Test Your Understanding 1.9
With SDLC, determining software requirements from the user(s) is typically included in the _____ phase.
A. planning
B. analysis
C. design
D. development

Test Your Understanding 1.10
With SDLC, actual coding and testing of a software project is typically done in the _____ phase.
A. planning
B. analysis
C. design
D. development

Test Your Understanding 1.11
With SDLC, drawing mockup screens for clients and developers is typically done in the _____ phase.
A. planning
B. analysis
C. design
D. development

Test Your Understanding 1.12
With SDLC, publishing the completed software project to the customer's computers is typically done in the _____ phase.

A. deploy
B. maintenance
C. design
D. development

Test Your Understanding 1.13
With SDLC, updating a currently used application is typically done in the _____ phase.
A. deploy
B. maintenance
C. design
D. development

1.5 Waterfall Approach

The team's work for the toy retailer is an example of the waterfall approach. This approach establishes well-structured phases that the developers can follow. At the end of each phase, the team produces one or more deliverables, such as the business plan and the system analysis report. There are also milestones to mark the end of each phase (usually the approval from the stakeholders). At the end of the deploy phase, the application is delivered to the customer as a whole, and the project can be closed. Figure 1.10 shows the sequence of phases in a typical waterfall approach.

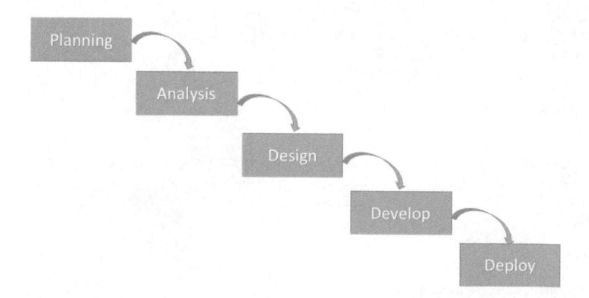

Figure 1.10 Traditional waterfall approach for software development.

Test Your Understanding 1.14
Stakeholders approving the business plan is an example of a project _____.
A. beginning point
B. closing point
C. milestone
D. deliverable

Test Your Understanding 1.15
In the waterfall approach, the approval from the stakeholders is often called _____.
A. green light
B. approved
C. start your engine
D. milestone

1.6 What's Wrong with the Waterfall?

The waterfall approach for systems development has been used for a long time and is still used by many businesses. However, over the years, professionals noted several problems.

The first major problem with the waterfall is the requirement for customers to know up-front what they want (Mikoluk, 2013). Customers usually have a general sense of what they want, but never a complete, detailed picture. As seen with Mr. Lincoln, many customers may know what they want at the beginning, but change their minds after seeing and running the application. By then, it is often too late for the development team to make any changes. In other words, customers won't see the finished application until it is done, which makes adjustments difficult. The Waterfall approach also assumes that all requirements have been specified in advance, which is unrealistic. That assumption, coupled with limited user involvement, reinforces the tendency of the waterfall model to lock in requirements too early, even after business conditions have changed.

The second problem has to do with the clear lines between roles in this approach. In other words, the waterfall method relies on specialists working together, which can be inefficient. System analysts do not know much about coding, and programmers may not care much about testing. A designer might plan something without knowing how difficult it is to code. As a result, it is neither realistic nor efficient to have such a team working on the same objectives. The best the team can do is cooperation. In cooperation, the role of customers was also narrowly defined (Kay, 2002). Users were often only involved in the requirements determination or analysis phases of the project. Quality assurance people also get paid according to how many bugs are found, so they are inclined towards more bugs in the product. What the team needs is collaboration, not cooperation.

The third problem is that the waterfall makes it hard to backtrack. Once the next phase starts, the previous phase cannot be changed since project managers need to freeze the design at a particular point so programmers can begin to code. This becomes problematic when customers want to change with business conditions during the development process. Additionally, the amount of effort spent on implementing a specific design makes it difficult to change once it is developed (Valacich and George, 2017).

Test Your Understanding 1.16
Which of the following is a major problem with the waterfall?
A. The customers should know how to program in at least one language.
B. There exists a clear line between roles such as analyst, designer, and programmer.
C. The team cannot plan for the next phase.
D. The project managers have too much power.

Test Your Understanding 1.17

Which of the following is NOT a major problem of the waterfall approach for software development?
A. Locking in requirements too early.
B. Too much repeating work.
C. Clear lines between roles.
D. Once the next phase starts, the previous phase(s) cannot be changed

1.7 What is Agile Methodology?

The agile methodology is a different way to achieve the same goals as the waterfall methodology.

The agile approach breaks the project into smaller pieces and then adds the pieces together in an order similar to the waterfall phases. However, since the project is now divided into smaller pieces, phases are no longer clearly segregated, and pieces of the project can instead be completed concurrently as feasible. How does this simple change dramatically affect the success of software development?

As stated in Section 1.6, there are three major problems with the traditional waterfall approach. The first problem is that customers cannot predict everything they need before development starts. Agile, on the other hand, develops a small part of the software based on the known requirements in less time. Then the software is shown to the customers, who can give feedback and more requirements. By completing the software in small increments, customers are better able to visualize the final product and provide a more thorough list of requirements. With small pieces, there's also less documentation to work on.

The second problem concerns the clear lines between team roles, which make collaboration difficult. In waterfall, teams consist of specialists who focus solely on their own role. With agile, team members are expected to be familiar with the entire process, on top of having his or her own expertise. You can think of the team as a small business, where even the owner has multiple roles, such as procurement manager, customer service, and marketing manager. When necessary, an agile team can also seek help from a subject-matter expert (SME).

Finally, as stated in the third problem, it is difficult to go back and make adjustments in the waterfall. Since the agile approach works in small pieces, fine tuning is incorporated along the way, and there is less of a need to "go back". Any changes that are needed will be reflected in the next 'pieces'.

Figure 1.11 shows such an approach. You should compare Figure 1.10 and 1.11 and see the differences between the two approaches.

Figure 1.11 Agile approach to software development.

A sprint in agile is defined as the whole process of building one or more small "pieces" of the application. Every sprint has a deliverable. A deliverable can be any piece of functional software. Each sprint includes all planning, analysis, design, coding/testing, and deploying steps, but in a very different way than waterfall. You will see the differences throughout the book when you learn more about agile.

Test Your Understanding 1.18
How does agile solve the problem of locking in requirements too early?
A. Requirements are not necessary in agile.
B. Requirements are only needed at the end of each sprint.
C. Requirements can be added after the customers see how some features work.
D. Requirements are created by the development team.

Test Your Understanding 1.19
How does agile solve the problem of too clear lines between team roles?
A. Each member plays multiple roles.
B. Take away the lines.
C. Developing small pieces does not require more than one person.
D. All roles are played by subject matter experts (SME).

Test Your Understanding 1.20
How does agile solve the problem of "going back"?
A. In agile, each piece is so small that there is no need to go back.
B. Agile makes it impossible to go back.
C. Agile only allows one team member to go back if necessary.
D. Agile members can go back at any time.

Test Your Understanding 1.21
In agile, the process of working on each smaller increments of an application is called a _____.
A. method
B. sprint
C. development
D. task

1.8 Agile is an Umbrella Term

Throughout the years, different companies and developers have created their own methodologies to avoid the problems of the traditional waterfall, as you've learned in section 1.6. Eventually, these developers decided to have a meeting to exchange their ideas and philosophies. In 2001, seventeen of them held a meeting at Snowbird, Utah. They formed the Agile Alliance group, whose mission was to promote the agile software development approach. They summarized the common characteristics of their approach and came up with four values and twelve principles (http://agilemanifesto.org/), which they called the Agile Manifesto.

The methodologies the practitioners used before the meeting (some are still in use today) include Scrum, extreme programming, Kanban, lean software development, crystal methodology, Dynamic Systems Development Methodology (DSDM), and Feature-Driven Development (FDD). This book will focus on Scrum, the most popular of all, and also briefly mention extreme programming and Kanban along the way.

Test Your Understanding 1.22

Which of the following is NOT one of the agile methodologies?
A. Scrum
B. eXtreme Programming

C. Kanban
D. C#

1.9 What are the Four Values of Agile?

The four values actually involve eight values. The purpose of the other four values is to show the importance of the four on the left in Figure 1.12

Figure 1.12 Four values of the Agile Manifesto

The first value, 'Individuals and Interactions', emphasizes the importance of the people, not the processes or the tools, that develop the software. It is equally important that the team work together through interaction and communication to reach their goal. This value suggests that people can choose their own way to develop software instead of following certain work procedures.

The second value, 'Working Software', stresses that the end product of the development is the software, not the documentation. Documentation is a helper, not the end result.

The third value, 'Customer Collaboration', highlights that customers and the development team have the same goal. The only way to achieve the goal is through collaboration. In the traditional approach, the customer requirements are usually documented in the contract and the team often wastes time negotiating the scope of the project.

The fourth value, 'Responding to Change', underlines the fact that change is not avoidable. While a plan is good, a plan is still based on a prediction of the future, which is often not accurate. In such a case, the plan needs to be updated. Continuous planning improves the chances of success. Change should be part of the plan. This allows the team to check the changes, get feedback and make revisions. Such practice delivers more valuable software for the customers. As shown in Figure 1.10, the traditional plan is made early in the project and can thus be a nightmare to follow. However, even though changes are unavoidable, agile does not support daily changes in software development. In agile, change is typically made between sprints, not while a sprint is in progress.

Test Your Understanding 1.23
Which of the following is a correct statement about agile?
A. In agile, how things are done is more important than who does the things.
B. In agile, teams do not need to write any documentation so time can be saved for coding.
C. In agile, customers and the development team cooperate for the same goal.
D. In agile, responding to change is more important than following the plan.

1.10 What are the Twelve Principles in Agile?

The complete list of the twelve principles is available at http://agilemanifesto.org/principles.html. In this section, we will summarize them in five points:

1. Working software should be delivered frequently instead of as one big software delivered at the end of the project. Using our C# example in this chapter, instead of completing the whole application at once, you would write the code that can display "Welcome to Agile" first. After you make this message display correctly, you add code to make the program beep. After you make the program beep, you add code to make the background green. With this approach, if anything goes wrong, it is easy to identify and fix it. Also, if the customers want something different, it is easy to accommodate.

2. The purpose of software development is to meet customer requirements. We should allow customers room to change their mind. For example, when they see the background color is green, they may want to make the font text color to be red for better contrast. The development team should have no difficulty adding that, even though the customer did not mention font color at the beginning. On the other hand, you should also work closely with the customer to cut costly changes that can be avoided.

3. The quality of the software depends on the development team. The team should be "self-organizing", meaning that they can work toward the common goal with great autonomy. The lines between the roles are blurred. Team members learn from each other. They work as a team, not as a sum of the individuals.

4. Continuous improvement is critical to the success of the team. They learn from their own experiences. What worked well? What didn't work? They learn from innovations in the field, and challenge themselves for better performance.

5. Simplicity can help one avoid many problems in software development and save money. Just make the software solve the business problems without the extra bells and whistles that the customers did not request.

Test Your Understanding 1.24
Frequent delivery of software allows better _____.
A. communication
B. rest for the team
C. customers
D. contract to be settled

Test Your Understanding 1.25
Which of the following statements is NOT correct about agile?
A. In agile, change requests from the customer are welcome.
B. The agile team should be "self-organizing", meaning that they can work toward the common goal with great autonomy.
C. The agile team should not be affected by the innovations in the field.
D. In agile working software should be delivered frequently in order to get timely customer feedback.

1.11 Chapter Summary

In this chapter, you learned that computers follow instructions written in a programming language. In C#, the statements are grouped into methods, methods are grouped into classes, and classes are grouped into namespace. You also learned how to use built-in classes and their methods to write your own statements.

Also in this chapter, you learned the phases in the traditional waterfall software development approach and compared it to the new agile approach. The chapter ended with a brief explanation of the Agile Manifesto.

1.12 References

Mikoluk, K. (2013), Agile Vs. Waterfall: Evaluating The Pros And Cons, Available at https://blog.udemy.com/agile-vs-waterfall/ accessed November 15, 2016.

Valacich, J. and George, J. (2017), Modern Systems Analysis and Design 8th Edition, Pearson, Boston.

1.13 Solutions to Programming Challenges

Programming Challenge 1.1

```
Console.ForegroundColor = ConsoleColor.Red;
Console.WriteLine("Welcome to Agile!");
Console.Beep();
Console.BackgroundColor = ConsoleColor.Green;
Console.WriteLine("Welcome again!");
Task.Delay(3000).Wait();
Console.Clear();
```

1.14 Solutions to Test Your Understanding

1.1 A; 1.2 C; 1.3 C; 1.4 A; 1.5 C; 1.6 B; 1.7 C; 1.8 A; 1.9 B; 1.10 D; 1.11 C; 1.12 A; 1.13 B; 1.14 C; 1.15 D; 1.16 B; 1.17 B; 1.18 C; 1.19 A; 1.20 A; 1.21 B; 1.22 D; 1.23 D; 1.24 A; 1.25 C;

Chapter 2: C# Statements and Agile Characteristics

2.1 What Is a Variable?

As you learned in Chapter 1, to program is to write instructions by following C# syntax. Sometimes, a value you need in the instruction may not be known at the time of programming or has changed over time. You use a variable to be a placeholder for an unknown value or change the value stored in a variable. Instructions in a program can reference and manipulate a variable. Additionally, variables make instructions more readable to programmers. A variable is a reserved space in computer memory that is used to store things like values. It is a named memory location to temporarily store data.

For example, in the last chapter, you displayed "Welcome to Agile" on the screen. What if you want to display "Welcome to C#"? You can use a variable to store the value you want to welcome and let the user decide what value to put in that variable. You can reference the value stored in the variable in many instructions.

Another example, if you want to calculate the square of a number that the user enters, you can use a variable, say x. Then you can calculate the square of x as x*x. The result value will depend on what value the user enters for x. This way your program is more powerful and flexible.

Test Your Understanding 2.1

In programming, a _____ can be used to store some value for later use.

A. variable

B. C#

C. storage

D. container

Example 2.1

Problem:

Write a program that asks the user for the name, and then displays the "Welcome to Agile, your name" message on the console screen. "Your name" will be replaced by the name user entered.

Solution:

Start a new console app in Visual Studio called Chapter2Example1. Save it to the Agile folder on your desktop (you followed the instructions and created the Agile folder in Chapter 1). With the default Program.cs open in the window, replace the default code with the following lines:

```
File   Edit   View   Git   Project   Build   Debug   Test   Analyze   Tools   Extensions

Debug  -  Any CPU  -  ▶ Chapter2Example

C# Chapter2Example1

1       // prompt user for a name
2       Console.WriteLine("Enter your name: ");
3       // store the user entered value in a variable
4       string name = Console.ReadLine();
5       // compose and display a message
6       Console.WriteLine("Welcome to Agile, " + name);
```

Figure 2.1 Code for Example 2.1

Explanation:

Line 1 starts with // which indicates this line is a comment. The C# compiler will ignore such lines. But, it helps programmers understand the code.

Line 4 ignores the green underline for now. The ReadLine() method of Console class will read the value the user enters from the keyboard. The user must press the "Enter" key for the end of the value. Line 6 uses the "+" operator to concatenate the string "Welcome to Agile, " and the value stored in the variable "name".

Click on the green start button to run it. Type in your name when prompted and you should see "Welcome to Agile, your name". Push the enter key to close the program.

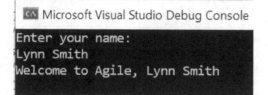

Figure 2.2 Sample output of Chapter 2 Example 1.

Variable naming rules:

A variable in C# can contain letters, numbers, and underscores only, and the first character cannot be a number. No spacing is allowed, and you cannot use the C# reserved keywords, such as Main, or abstract.

Additionally, a variable name is case sensitive, e.g. 'name' and 'Name' are different.

Test Your Understanding 2.2
Which of the following is NOT a legal variable name for C#?
A. studentName
B. student_name
C. studentName1
D. 2studentName

Test Your Understanding 2.3
Variable names are case _____ in C#, which means 'student' and 'Student' are treated differently.
A. sensitive
B. dependent
C. specific
D. based

2.2 What Is Data Type?

Note that in the code example above, Figure 2.1, string (a data type) was added right before the variable 'name'. Using a data type helps the compiler reserve the right size of memory space for the variable value.

Other commonly used simple data types include *int* (for storing whole numbers, such as 5 or 12), *double* (for storing floating point numbers, such as 3.14), and *decimal* (for storing floating point numbers with higher accuracy; you will use this type for money values). The data type *char* is used for single characters, and the data type *bool* is used to store a Boolean value, such as true or false.

A literal value, such as 3.14, will be treated as a double data type. To make it as a decimal data type, use 3.14m. The suffix indicates a decimal data type. See Programming Challenge 2.2 solution for an example.

One important thing to know about data type is its value range. For example, for *int*, the valid range of values is from -2,147,483,648 to 2,147,483,647. If you try to store a value out of that range, an error will occur. For a complete list of built-in data types, visit https://msdn.microsoft.com/en-us/library/ya5y69ds.aspx. Just click on the type name on the page to view more details.

Test Your Understanding 2.4
In C#, the *int* data type can be used to store any whole number.
A. True
B. False

Test Your Understanding 2.5
In C#, if you want to store the value of a student's letter grade (one of 'A', 'B', 'C', 'D', 'F', 'I', 'P'), what is the most appropriate data type?
A. int
B. double
C. char
D. string

Test Your Understanding 2.6
What is the difference between a double and a decimal data type in C#?
A. double works for integers.
B. decimal works for integers.

C. double has higher accuracy.

D. decimal has higher accuracy.

Test Your Understanding 2.7

If students take a course that can only receive the grade of pass or fail, what is the most appropriate data type for storing the grade?

A. double

B. decimal

C. char

D. bool

2.3 What is an Operator?

Computers are good at calculations, so you can use operators to add, subtract, multiply, and divide, etc., on numbers and variables. Let's see an example.

Example 2.2

Problem:

A bag holds 50 candies. The calorie information on the bag indicates that there are 25 servings in each bag and that a serving equals 100 calories. Write a program that lets the user enter the number of candies he or she ate and then displays the number of total calories consumed.

Solution:

Start a console app in Visual Studio called Chapter2Example2. Save it to the Agile folder on your desktop (you followed the instructions and created the folder in Chapter 1). With the default Program.cs open in the window, replace the default two lines with the following:

```
1      // use constant variables to hold values
2      const int NUMBER_OF_CANDIES_IN_BAG = 50;
3      const int SERVINGS_PER_BAG = 25;
4      const int CALORIES_PER_SERVING = 100;
5      // first, compute how many candies per serving
6      double numberOfCandiesPerServing =
7          NUMBER_OF_CANDIES_IN_BAG / SERVINGS_PER_BAG;
8      // next, compute how many calories per candy
9      double caloriesPerCandy =
10         CALORIES_PER_SERVING / numberOfCandiesPerServing;
11     // prompt user for number of candies consumed
12     Console.WriteLine("How many candies did you eat?");
13     // get the number from the user and store it in a variable
14     int candiesAte = int.Parse(Console.ReadLine());
15     // compute how many calories consumed
16     double caloriesConsumed = candiesAte * caloriesPerCandy;
17     // display the result on console screen
18     Console.WriteLine($"You have consumed {caloriesConsumed} calories.");
```

Figure 2.3 Code for Chapter2 Example 2.

Explanation:

Lines 2 to 4 declare and initialize three constant variables. Unlike a regular variable, the value stored in a constant variable cannot be changed by statements later on. It is a better practice to use constant when you don't want the value to be changed.

Lines 6 and 7 can be in one line. It is broken here into two for a better screenshot. The "/" is a division operator used in C#.

Line 14 converts a string value to an int value so that we can apply multiplication on it in Line 16. Most data type has a Parse() method that allows you to convert a string value to a desired type. Note that only a number like "2" can be converted to an integer. You cannot convert "Two" to an integer by the Parse() method. Also note that Console.ReadLine() always returns a string type even if you typed in "2".

Line 16, the "*" is a multiplication operator.

Line 18 puts a "$" sign in front of a string to indicate this is an interpolated string which you can insert a variable in the string within a pair of curly braces. You can also format the variable, e.g. {caloriesConsumed:N2} will make the value displayed in two decimal places. or{somevariable:C} will make the value displayed as currency.

Figure 2.4 Sample output for Chapter2 Example 2.

Test Your Understanding 2.8

What is the difference between the following two statements?

1) int numberOfCandiesInBag = 50;

2) const int numberOfCandiesInBag = 50;

A. 1) is a simpler statement without the keyword const and is thus recommended.

B. 2) will not allow later statements in the program to accidentally change the value and is thus recommended.

C) 1) and 2) are the same.

D) Only one of the statements is correct.

Programming Challenge 2.1

Lynn's Pizza Restaurant needs an application to calculate the number of slices a pizza can be divided into. Your application should let the user enter the radius of the pizza in inches, then display how many slices this pizza can be cut assuming one slice is no less than 15 square inches. (Hint, the area of a whole pizza is calculated by Area = πr^2, where π is 3.14 and r is the radius. You may also use Math.PI for 3.14 where Math is a prebuilt class and PI is one of its properties. A property of Math called Floor can remove the decimal portion of a number.)

Example 2.3

Problem:

Write a program that prints the minimum number of quarters, dimes, nickels, and pennies that a customer should get back as change. Ask the user for a change amount, such as 1.23, or 0.54. Then the program should display the number of each type of coin needed.

Solution:

Start a console app in Visual Studio called Chapter2Example3. Save it to the Agile folder on your

desktop (you followed the instructions and created the folder in Chapter 1). With the default

Program.cs open in the window, replace the default code with like the following:

```
1    // prompt user for amount of change
2    Console.WriteLine("Enter change amount:");
3    // store the amount in a variable
4    decimal changeAmount = decimal.Parse(Console.ReadLine());
5    // convert amount in whole number of cents
6    int changeInCents = (int)(changeAmount * 100);
7    // compute number of quarters (25 cents) needed
8    int numberOfQuarters = changeInCents / 25;
9    // computer the remainder
10   int remainderAfterQuarters = changeInCents % 25;
11   // compute number of dimes (10 cents) needed
12   int numberOfDimes = remainderAfterQuarters / 10;
13   // compute the remainder
14   int remainderAfterDimes = remainderAfterQuarters % 10;
15   // compute number of nickles (5 cents) needed
16   int numberOfNickles = remainderAfterDimes / 5;
17   // compute remainder, this is number of pennies needed
18   int remainderAfterNickles = remainderAfterDimes % 5;
19   int numberOfPennies = remainderAfterNickles;
20   // display reult
21   Console.WriteLine($"Number of Quarters: {numberOfQuarters}");
22   Console.WriteLine($"Number of Dimes: {numberOfDimes}");
23   Console.WriteLine($"Number of Nickless: {numberOfNickles}");
24   Console.WriteLine($"Number of Pennies: {numberOfPennies}");
```

Figure 2.5 Code for Chapter 2 Example 3.

Figure 2.6 Sample output for Chapter 2 Example 3.

Explanation:

Line 6 explicitly casts a decimal type variable to an int type. It will remove any decimal places. See what happens if you remove the second pair of parentheses. It will remove the decimal in change amount before multiplication.

Line 10 introduces another useful arithmetic operator: module (% sign), which is a way to calculate the remainder of an integer division.

Programming Challenge 2.2

Lynn's Pizza Restaurant also sells cookies. One cookie costs 12 cents. A dozen cookies cost $1.20. Any number of cookies less than a dozen costs 12 cents each. For example, 10 cookies would cost $1.20, 11 cookies would cost $1.32, 12 cookies would cost $1.20, 13 cookies would cost $1.32, and 30 cookies would cost $3.12. Write a program to ask the user for the number of cookies, then display the total cost.

```
C:\ Microsoft Visual Studio Debug Console
How many cookies do you buy?
30
The total cost for 30 cookies is $3.12
```

Figure 2.7 Sample output for Programming Challenge 2.2.

Programming Challenge 2.3

Smith's Fast Food sells burgers, fries, and drinks only. The price of a burger is $1.50. The price of a serving of French fries is $1.20. A cup of drink is $1.00. Write a program that asks the user for the number of items for each food, then displays the total cost (Assuming no sales tax.). Remember to use const for the unit price of each food.

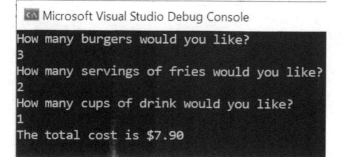

```
C:\ Microsoft Visual Studio Debug Console
How many burgers would you like?
3
How many servings of fries would you like?
2
How many cups of drink would you like?
1
The total cost is $7.90
```

Figure 2.8 Sample output for Programming Challenge 2.3.

Programming Challenge 2.4

Lynn's Pizza Restaurant needs a tip calculator for customers to calculate tips. The program will prompt the user to enter a purchase amount. Then, the program will calculate and display tips at 15%, 18%, and 20%, as well as display the total cost of the meal including the tip. You should use const for those tip percentages instead of literal values. We will assume there is no state sales tax.

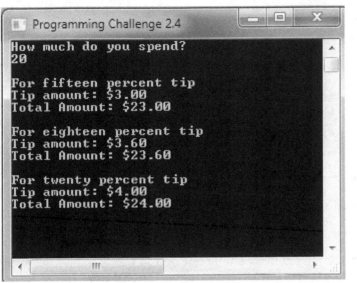

Figure 2.9 Programming Challenge 2.4 sample output.

2.4 Characteristics of Agile

Agile practice is very different from traditional practices. There are five differences (Ashmore and Runyan, 2014):

1. Self-Organizing Teams

The traditional software development team has a project manager. The agile team has no project managers and is trusted by the management to operate successfully. Unlike a non-agile project team, an agile team establishes its own norms and rules. Team members have a lot of autonomy regarding their work.

Furthermore, instead of being assigned tasks to work on, team members get to select their tasks and how they want to do the job. (Of course, these tasks are to accomplish the user stories provided by customers through the product owner.)

2. Continuous Improvement (solving your own problems)

In agile, each team member is responsible for ensuring that problems from a past or current iteration are not carried into the next. This creates a higher level of engagement from employees, because they will be responsible for any problems that arise.

In the past, team members relied on the project manager to resolve issues. In agile, the team is empowered and encouraged to seek out answers and improvements on its own.

3. Quick customer feedback

In a non-agile environment, the team won't deliver the software to the customer until the whole application is finished. This makes customer feedback difficult, considering the relatively long process. Furthermore, the final delivered application might be very different from what the customers envisioned at the start. Customers may also have changed their minds during the process.

In an agile environment, the team will demo the completed part of the software to the customer at the end of each sprint. A sprint only delivers an increment instead of the whole application. Agile utilizes small increments and more frequent feedback. As a result, when all pieces are put together, the software is more likely to meet the customer's vision.

4. Blurring the lines between roles in a team

Before agile, a software development team would have needed to hire specialists, such as analysts, programmers, and testers. In the agile setting, there are no C# programmers or testers; everyone is a team member. That is one reason why this book merges agile and C#: so by the end of this book, you will be able to practice agile with actual software development as an agile team member.

For example, in a traditional setting, a tester would not start working until the programmer completed the code, and the programmer would consider his or her work completed once the tested began. This often resulted in poor quality and subsequent finger pointing.

In an agile setting, where the programmers and testers collaborate to develop high quality software, only the end result matters. It is the whole team's responsibility to complete the software.

Agile teams usually include members with a broad skill set, such as analyzing, designing, programming, and testing. However, members are expected to participate in any role the team needs them to fill (Highsmith, 2002). This situation differs from the traditional waterfall structured environments, where teams often specialize according to function (e.g., analyst, designer, developer, tester) (Nerur et al, 2005). In waterfall, team members often have different responsibilities and titles across organizations.

In agile, systems analysts might perform programming and design responsibilities in their job even though it is not required of them. A developer might also perform programming, testing, and configuration management tasks that would be fragmented in a traditional setting.

5. Physical Workspace

The physical workspace in agile is different by the removal of cubical borders. The close proximity of team members allows easy and quick communication. This increases efficiency and can also improve the quality of the software, though some employees may feel a lack of privacy.

Test Your Understanding 2.9
Which of the following statements about agile is true?
1) In an agile team, members get to pick any task they want, even their own project from another company.
2) In an agile team, there is no project manager role.
A. 1) only
B. 2) only
C. both 1) and 2)
D. neither 1) nor 2)

Test Your Understanding 2.10
Which of the following statements about agile is true?
1) In an agile team, compared to a traditional team, members get more frequent feedback.
2) In an agile team, every member is equally capable at analyzing, designing, programming, and testing.
A. 1) only
B. 2) only
C. both 1) and 2)
D. neither 1) nor 2)

2.5 Why Agile Does Not Work All the Time for All Companies

Agile methodologies have increased software development success rates, improved software quality, and shortened the time it takes to reach the market. It also enhances the motivation and productivity of the development team (Ghani et al., 2015, Rigby et. Al, 2016). What makes agile so successful?

Research on agile success (Sammon et al., 2009) started with ten factors and narrowed it down to four. These factors make the difference between success and failure (Dhir et al, 2019).

1. Organizational and Reporting Structure

In agile, work cannot be done alone. Whether success is achieved can be determined by organizational structure. An example of a successful structure is organic organization (Bennis, 1969), which is identified as having little job specialization, few layers of management, decentralized decision making, and little direct supervision. These attributes allow flexibility and adaptability. An organization with organic structure is more likely to succeed with an agile approach.

2. Organizational Process

Much like how the organizational structure can affect agile success, the organizational process does too. The organizational process includes work environment standards that support organizational learning and process improvement by promoting sharing of the best practices learned across the organization (CMMI Product Team, 2007).

Due to different mindsets, a process such as the Capability Maturity Model, which is used to develop and refine an organization's software development process, may conflict with agile methodologies.

3. Documentation Requirements

Even though agile methodologies do not prohibit documentation, the more time the team spend on documentation, the less time they have to work on the software. Thus, the documentation requirements affect the success of an agile approach. The documentation should be kept at a minimum.

4. Layout of Workspace

Similar to item 5 of the agile characteristics discussed earlier in this chapter, layout of workspace is an important factor for the success of agile. While both an open plan office and a clustered cubicle approach are popular among IT companies, some experts in agile suggest some kind of isolated room for a single team. This allows members to chat freely and promotes communication and teamwork. Furthermore, this layout facilitates bonding without the interference of other teams (Muldoon, 2014).

Test Your Understanding 2.11
Which of the following is NOT a success factor for agile approach?
A. Team cellphone usage policy
B. Organizational and reporting structure
C. Organizational process
D. Documentation requirement

Test Your Understanding 2.12
An organization with _____ structure is more likely to succeed with an agile approach.
A. hierarchical
B. functional
C. matrix
D. organic

For organizations that are new to agile software development, Cooke (2011) suggested five steps to success.

1. Choosing the right kick-off point. Many developers switched to agile because they were struggling with their current project. That may not be the right time. They should take a step back and try to understand agile better, get prepared, and then start. The best time to start agile is when the team is well prepared and ready for the agile approach.

2. Choosing the right project(s). For example, a project that is not burdened by any legacy systems or pre-existing management techniques might be a good 'first' agile project. The success of the first project is often critical for persuading management to adopt the agile approach.

3. Choosing the right methodologies and practices. As you will learn in the next section, there is more

than one flavor of agile approach. The organization culture, team member backgrounds, and the project can all affect the appropriate methodologies and practices. You can combine different types of agile or even create one for yourself as long as you follow the agile principles.

4. Choosing the right method of introduction. Like many other practices, agile can be introduced top down or bottom up. With top down, you have the organizational mandate on using agile. This approach is usually easier for the team because the champions are often the top management. With bottom up, you might be the champion.

5. Avoiding common traps which include undermining agile principles, insufficient communication and training, and using agile as a doctrine instead of a tool.

Test Your Understanding 2.13
For organizations that are new to agile software development, Cooke (2011) suggested five steps to success. Which of the following is NOT a step?
A. Choosing the right kick-off point
B. Choosing the right project(s)
C. Choosing the right project manager(s)
D. Choosing the right methodologies and practices

2.6 Types of Agile.

As you have learned in chapter one, agile is an umbrella term. In this section, you will discover a few major types of agile methodologies, namely scrum, extreme programming (XP), and Kanban. In the rest of the book, we may not always differentiate which type of agile is used.

2.6.1 Scrum

Scrum is a lightweight framework. It is simple to understand, but difficult to master. Unlike the traditional waterfall project management methodology that requires comprehensive documentation and heavyweight processes, scrum is lightweight and focuses on working software and team collaborations. Its organization, roles, events, and artifacts are easy to understand, but applying it to the field can be difficult.

Teams are free to develop different processes and techniques as long as they follow the rules, roles, and events of the scrum framework. As a result, there are many flavors of scrum.

The term 'scrum' was introduced by Takeuchi and Nonaka (1986) regarding business operations. They explained that projects using small cross-functional teams historically produced the best results. They compared these high-performance teams to "scrum" formations in Rugby.

Scrum for software development was introduced in 1993 by Jeff Sutherland at Easel Corporation, using the study by Takeuchi and Nonaka (1986) as the basis for adopting their analogy as the name of the process for software development.

Scrum is based on the empirical process control theory (Viscardi, 2013). According to this theory, knowledge comes from experience, and decisions should be made according to what is known. It has three foundations (Crisan et al., 2015): transparency, inspection, and adaptation.

The transparency foundation indicates that the software developed should be visible to all stakeholders. Inspection specifies that experienced inspectors should check the scrum artifacts against the team goals on a regular basis. Adaptation suggests that if any differences are found in the inspection, the team should adjust the related processes or materials.

Scrum includes three roles, five events, and three artifacts. These will be covered in more detail in later chapters. Scrum is the most popular agile practice. This book mostly follows scrum practice.

Test Your Understanding 2.14
The _____ foundation of scrum indicates that the software developed should be visible to all stakeholders.

A. Transparency
B. Collaboration
C. Inspection
D. Adaptation

Test Your Understanding 2.15
Scrum is _____ and focuses on working software and team _____.
A. lightweight, collaborations
B. heavyweight, collaborations
C. lightweight, corporations
D. heavyweight, corporations

Test Your Understanding 2.16
Which of the following is NOT a scrum foundation?
A. Transparency
B. Collaboration
C. Inspection
D. Adaptation

Test Your Understanding 2.17
Scrum framework includes ____ roles, ____ events, and ____ artifacts.
A. 1, 2, 3
B. 3, 4, 5
C. 3, 2, 5
D. 3, 5, 3

2.6.2 Extreme Programming (XP)

Extreme Programming (XP) is another popular agile methodology (Amir et al, 2013). It requires that customers be part of the team. It uses a process similar to sprint called 'iterations'. It has the following four characteristics: continuous integration, user story, team velocity, and pair programming.

1. Continuous Integration: XP requires frequent releases and very short development cycles. A cycle can be as short as one day. The idea of small iterations is the same as scrum's sprints, save for the length, which is one day compared to a sprint's two weeks.

2. User story: These are software requirements written in a specific format. It is short and can fit on an index card. The story serves as a conversation between the customer and the development team, not a

specification from the customer for the team. An example of a user story is "As the owner of the company, I want to be able to check the up-to-date inventory data so that I can better manage my business". Based on this user story, the development team may ask if the owner wants to see one inventory item at a time by searching or displaying all inventory at once. This starts the conversation and helps both customers and the team understand the requirements better. The size of a user story is measured by story points. Every user story has story points estimated by the development team to reflect how much effort is needed to complete the story.

3. Team Velocity: This is a way to measure how much work can be done in a certain amount of time by the team. This velocity is measured by the number of story points. For example, a team doesn't usually say how many stories they can complete in one iteration, but rather how many story points they can complete. It is done this way because not all user stories require the same amount of effort.

4. Pair Programming: This is used to help produce high quality software. In this technique, two team members take turns controlling the keyboard. While one member types, the other one watches and brainstorms. This technique works well when a programmer and a tester form a team. Code does not need to be completed then inspected. The code is checked as it is typed into the program.

Test Your Understanding 2.18
Frequent releases and very short development cycles describe which characteristic of extreme programming?
A. continuous integration
B. pair programming
C. user story
D. team velocity

Test Your Understanding 2.19
Which characteristic of extreme programming is kind of similar to a scrum sprint?
A. continuous integration
B. pair programming
C. user story
D. team velocity

Test Your Understanding 2.20

Which of the following is NOT a characteristic of XP?
A. continuous integration
B. transparency
C. user story
D. team velocity

Test Your Understanding 2.21
Two team members working on the same task to increase product quality is which characteristic of extreme programming?
A. continuous integration
B. user story
C. team velocity
D. pair programming

2.6.3 Kanban

The Kanban methodology has three characteristics (Ashmore and Runyan, 2014).

1. Visualizing the workflow: A Kanban board is used to map the workflow in columns based on the status of a task. The task is often written on sticky notes and posted on a column in the board or simply on the wall.

2. Limits on works in progress (WIP): It is easy to see how many tasks are in each stage (a stage = a column on the Kanban board). With a limited number of tasks in each stage, it is easy to identify the bottlenecks.

Limiting works in progress is good for quality, a topic in chapter 7. With a limited number of tasks, the team can focus on solving any problems they may have without working overtime. So, when the number of bugs accumulate, the whole team would stop writing new code and focus on fixing the bugs.

3. Measure the lead time: With smooth flow of work, it is easy to discover the time it takes to complete a task from start to finish.

Test Your Understanding 2.22
Which of the following is NOT a characteristic of Kanban methodology?
A. continuous integration
B. visualizing the workflow
C. limiting works in progress
D. measuring the lead time

Test Your Understanding 2.23
In Kanban methodology, it is easy to identify the _____ because the number of tasks in progress is limited.
A. shortest
B. longest
C. bottleneck
D. winner task

2. 7 Chapter Summary

In this chapter, you learned how to write C# statements by using variables and operators. You should follow rules for naming variables and select the appropriate data type for each variable. There are many more data types and operators used in C# that can be looked up online.

You also learned the characteristics of agile and the success factors. You should know there is more than just one type of agile. In fact, there are many hybrid types, such as scrumban, which combines both scrum and Kanban.

2.8 References

Amir, M., Khan, K., Khan, A., and Khan, M. (2013), An Appraisal of Agile Software Development Process, International Journal of Advanced Science & Technology 58, pp. 57-86.

Ashmore, S. and Runyan, K. (2014), Introduction to Agile Methods 1st Edition, Boston, Addison-Wesley Professional.

Bennis, W. (1969). The Mature of Organizational Development. Reading, Mass,: Addison-Wesley.

CMMI Product Team, (2007), CMMI® for Acquisition, Version 1.2, Carnegie Mellon University, Software Engineering Institute, http://chrguibert.free.fr/cmmi12/cmmi-acq/text/index.php, Visited Nov. 18, 2016.

Crisan, E., Belieiu, I. and Ilies, . (2015), The Place of Agile in Management Science - A Literature Review, Managerial Challenges of the Contemporary Society, 8: 1, pp. 62-65.

Dhir, S., Kumar, D., & Singh, V. B. (2019). Success and failure factors that impact on project implementation using agile software development methodology. In Software Engineering (pp. 647-654). Springer, Singapore.

Ghani, I., Bello, M., and Bagiwa, I. (2015) Survey-based Analysis of Agile adoption on performance of IT organization, Journal of Korean Society for Internet Information, October, 16(5), 87-92.

Highsmith, J. (2002). Agile software development ecosystems. Boston: Addison Wesley.

Muldoon, N. (2014), Building an Ideal Agile Team Workspace, http://www.velocitycounts.com/2014/01/building-best-agile-team-workspace/, Visited November 18, 2016Nerur, S., Mahapatra, R. K., & Mangalaraj, G. (2005). Challenges of migrating to agile methodologies. Communications of the ACM, 48(5), 72-78.

Rigby, D. K., Sutherland, J., and Takeuchi, H. (2016), Embracing Agile, Harvard Business Review 94(5), 40-50.

Sammon, D, McAvoy, J, and Owens, I. (2009), Agile Teams: Reflective Debate and Shared Understanding, Proceedings of the European Conference on Information Management & Evaluation, p535-543.

Sutherland, Jeff. (1995) Business Object Design and Implementation. 10th Annual Conference on Object-Oriented Programming Systems, Languages, and Applications Addendum to the Proceedings. *OOPS Messenger 6:4*:170-175. ACM/SIGPLAN October.

Takeuchi, H.; Nonaka, I. (1986), The new new product development game, Harvard Business Review. Jan/Feb, Vol. 64 Issue 1, p137-146

Viscardi, S. (2013), The Professional ScrumMaster's Handbook: A Collection of Tips, Tricks, and War Stories to Help THE Professional ScrumMaster Break the Chains of Traditional Organizatin and Management, Packt Publishing, Birmingham, U.K.

2.9 Solutions to Programming Challenges

Programming Challenge 2.1

```
// define slice size (each slice is 15 square inches)
const int SLICE_SIZE = 15;
// prompt user for the radius of the pizza
Console.WriteLine("Enter radius of the pizza (inches):");
// store the value in a variable
double radius = double.Parse(Console.ReadLine());
// compute the area of the pizza
double area = Math.PI * radius * radius;
// compute the number of slices
double numberOfSlice = area / SLICE_SIZE;
// display the result to the user
Console.WriteLine($"The pizza can be cut into {Math.Floor(numberOfSlice)} slices");
```

Programming Challenge 2.2

```
// set const values
const int DOZEN_COOKIES = 12;
const decimal DOZEN_COST = 1.2m;
const decimal SINGLE_COOKIE_COST = 0.12m;
// prompt user for number of cookies bought
Console.WriteLine("How many cookies do you buy?");
// store the value in a variable
int numberOfCookies = int.Parse(Console.ReadLine());
// divide the number by DOZEN_COOKIES to find how many dozens
int dozens = numberOfCookies / DOZEN_COOKIES;
// module to find the remainder
int dozenRemainder = numberOfCookies % DOZEN_COOKIES;
// calculate the cost, m converts a double value to a decimal value
decimal totalCost = dozens * DOZEN_COST + dozenRemainder * SINGLE_COOKIE_COST;
// display the total cost in currency format
Console.WriteLine($"The total cost for {numberOfCookies} cookies is {totalCost:C}");
```

2.10 Solutions to Test Your Understanding

2.1 A; 2.2 D; 2.3 A; 2.4 B; 2.5 C; 2.6 D; 2.7 D; 2.8 B; 2.9 B; 2.10 A; 2.11 A; 2.12 D; 2.13 C; 2.14 A;

2.15 A; 2.16 B; 2.17 D; 2.18 A; 2.19 A; 2.20 B; 2.21 D; 2.22 A; 2.23 C.

Chapter 3 C# Flow Control and Agile Roles

Chapter Learning Outcomes

3.1 Recognizing syntax for conditional statements

3.2 Recognizing syntax for repeating statements

3.3 Implementing conditional and repeating statements in problem solving

3.4 Recalling types of roles in agile

3.5 Recognizing major responsibilities for each role in agile

3.1 Conditional Statements

Computers follow instructions. So far, you've seen the instructions are sequential; one statement is executed after the other in the order they are presented. This limits the use of the program, since they cannot change the execution sequence. The real world often requires different statements to be executed when certain conditions are true. For example, if a student's score is 90 or higher, you may want to display a congratulations message, while other students receive the typical response.

3.1.1 If Statements

C# has conditional statements, including the 'if' statement. If a condition is true, a block of statements will be executed. If not, a different block of statements will be executed. The if statement allows you to check more than one condition with the "else if" statement.

Example 3.1

Problem:

Write an application that asks the user for a numeric score of a student's test. If the score is 90 or higher, display the message "Congratulations". Otherwise, display "Thank you for using the system."

Solution:

Start a console app in Visual Studio called Chapter3Example1. With the default Program.cs open in the code view, replace the default code with the following:

```
1     // prompt user for a score
2     Console.WriteLine("Enter a student score:");
3     // store the score in a variable
4     double score = double.Parse(Console.ReadLine());
5     // check to see if the score is 90 or higher
6     if(score >= 90)
7     {
8         Console.WriteLine("Congratulations!");
9     }
10    else
11    {
12        Console.WriteLine("Thanks for using the system.");
13    }
```

Figure 3.1 Code for Example 3.1

Click the green start button to run it. Type in a number less than 90 and press the enter to see "Thanks for using the system" on the console screen. Push enter to end the program.

Click the green start button again. This time, type in a number greater than or equal to 90 and push enter to see "Congratulations!" on the console screen. Push enter to end the program.

Explanation:

Lines 6 through 13 are an if statement, which includes a condition on Line 6. If the condition is evaluated to be true, the statements inside the braces block (only Line 8 in this case) are executed. Otherwise, the statements inside the else block will be executed (in this case, Line 12).

The 'else' part of an if statement is optional.

You can also add an "else if" statement to the if statement. For example, if you wanted to display "Good job!" for students who scored between 80 and 90, you can add the following instructions between Lines 9 and 10:

```
else if (score >= 80)
{
    Console.WriteLine("Good job!");
}
```

An if statement usually includes all statements you want to execute under certain conditions in a pair of braces as shown in Lines 7 and 9. However, some people prefer no braces when there is only one line of statement in the block. You are encouraged to use braces so that the code is more readable.

Test Your Understanding 3.1
C# allows your program to execute a block of statements only when certain _____ are true.
A. numbers
B. conditions
C. WriteLines
D. Consoles

Test Your Understanding 3.2
When a condition is true, an if statement can execute a block of statements inside a pair of _____. If there is only one statement in the block, the pair of _____.
A. parentheses, parentheses is optional
B. parentheses, parentheses is still required
C. curly braces, curly braces is optional
D. curly braces, curly braces is still required

Test Your Understanding 3.3
When executing the following if statement:
```
if(score >= 90)
{
    Console.WriteLine("Congratulations!");
}
if (score >= 80)
{
    Console.WriteLine("Good job!");
}
else
{
    Console.WriteLine("Thanks for using the system.");
}
```
For a score of 95, what is on the console screen?
A. Congratulations!
B. Good job!
C. Congratulations!
   Good job!
D. Thanks for using the system.

Programming Challenge 3.1

Write an application that prompts the user to enter two integers. Then displays a menu like this:
Enter 1, 2, or 3
1. Addition
2. Multiplication

3. Exit

After the user enters the selection (1, 2, or 3), the application will display the result based on user inputs and the menu selection.

3.1.2 Switch Statements

The switch statement is similar to the if statement in that it executes a block of code based on certain conditions. However, there are two major differences: 1) switch can test for multiple values of a test variable in one go, and thus executes faster than an if statement. For example, if you want to display the month in letters when given a number (ex. - February in response to '2'), a switch statement is faster than an if statement. 2) a switch statement is often more readable for more complex comparisons.

Example 3.2

Problem:

Write an application that prompts the user for an integer between 1 and 12. The application will display the corresponding name of the month in letters.

Solution:

Start a console app in Visual Studio called Chapter3Example2. With the default Program.cs open in the code view, replace the default lines with the following:

```
// prompt user for an integer between 1 and 12
Console.WriteLine("Enter a whole number between 1 and 12:");
// store the number
int numericMonth = int.Parse(Console.ReadLine());
// declare a variable to store month in word
string monthInWord;
switch (numericMonth)
{
   case 1:
     monthInWord = "January";
     break;
   case 2:
     monthInWord = "February";
     break;
   case 3:
     monthInWord = "March";
     break;
   case 4:
```

```
      monthInWord = "April";
      break;
    case 5:
      monthInWord = "May";
      break;
    case 6:
      monthInWord = "June";
      break;
    case 7:
      monthInWord = "July";
      break;
    case 8:
      monthInWord = "August";
      break;
    case 9:
      monthInWord = "September";
      break;
    case 10:
      monthInWord = "October";
      break;
    case 11:
      monthInWord = "November";
      break;
    case 12:
      monthInWord = "December";
      break;
    default:
      monthInWord = "That is not a whole number between 1 and 12";
      break;
}
Console.WriteLine(monthInWord);
```

Explanation:

A switch statement begins with a match expression (numericMonth in the example), followed by a series of case keywords. The case line indicates the match pattern, which can be a constant pattern (as in the example) or a relational pattern. If a match is found, the block of statements is executed. If no match is found, the execution will go to the "default" block. Remember to include the "break" keyword that indicates the end of a block.

You may combine multiple case pattern into one, like this:

```
    case 10:
    case 11:
    case 12:
      monthInWord = "October/November/December";
      break;
```

Test Your Understanding 3.4
A switch statement begins with a _____, followed by a series of _____ keywords.

A. match expression, switch
B. match expression, case
C. int value, switch
D. int value, case

Test Your Understanding 3.5
The if statement and switch statement are similar. Which of the following is a factor when you prefer to use a switch statement?
A. Performance and security
B. Performance and readability
C. Conciseness and security
D. Conciseness and readability

Programming Challenge 3.2

Write an application to prompt the user to enter an integer between 1 and 10, and have the application display the English word for that number. For example, if the user enters 5, the application will display 'five'.

3.2 Repeating Statements

In the last chapter, you learned how to tell computers what to do in sequential order. In the last section, you learned how to tell computers to execute only certain instructions when a condition is true. With conditional statements, you can branch the route of execution in more than one way. In many situations, sequential and conditional statements may not be enough. In Example 3.1, you might have noticed that it is inconvenient to run the program only once. How about modifying the code so that the program can run until the user wants to quit?

3.2.1 The 'while' Loop

A while loop will check a condition. If the condition is true, it will execute the statements in the block. If the condition is false, it will quit the loop. This is similar to the if statement. The difference is that an if statement only checks the condition once and executes the statement block once. The while loop will check the condition repeatedly and thus may execute the block of statements multiple times until the condition is false. It is very important that you are able to change the condition inside the execution block. Otherwise, the loop may go on infinitely.

Example 3.3

Problem:

Modify Example 3.1 so that it will prompt the user for a score and display the message based on the score. The application can repeat the prompt and display the message until the user enters a negative score.

Solution:

Start a console app in Visual Studio called Chapter3Example3. With the default Program.cs open in the code view, replace the default code with the following:

```
1     // prompt user for a score
2     Console.WriteLine("Enter a student score (-1 to terminate):");
3     // store the score in a variable
4     double score = double.Parse(Console.ReadLine());
5     // start a loop
6     while(score >= 0)
7     {
8         // check to see if the score is 90 or higher
9         if (score >= 90)
10        {
11            Console.WriteLine("Congratulations!");
12        }
13        else
14        {
15            Console.WriteLine("Thanks for using the system.");
16        }
17        // prompt user for another score
18        Console.WriteLine("Enter a student score (-1 to terminate):");
19        // store the score in the same variable, replacing the old one
20        score = double.Parse(Console.ReadLine());
21    }
```

Figure 3.4 Code for Example 3.3.

Execute the code. Type in a score less than 90 and see the message "Thanks for using the system." on the console screen. Next, type in a score greater than 90 and see the message "Congratulations!" on the console screen. You can repeat this as many times as you want. To end the program, enter any negative number. Press enter to end the program.

Explanation:

Line 6 starts a while loop, which is almost the same as an if statement. The while loop will check the condition again after the block of statements (from Lines 7 to 21) is executed versus an if statement, which will not check the condition again after the execution of the block.

What happens if you comment out (add // before a statement to make the compiler ignore it) Lines 18 and 20 in Figure 3.4? If the score entered is more than 90, you will see "Congratulations!" running forever because that's what it is supposed to do according to the code. That is called an infinite loop and is usually not what we want. So, make sure your code contains statements that can change the condition in the while statement (like the statement in Line 20, which can be negative) and thus make it possible to terminate the program.

Test Your Understanding 3.6
C# allows your program to _____ running a block of statements as long as certain conditions are true by using _____ loop.
A. selective, while
B. selective, if
C. repeat, while
D. repeat, if

Test Your Understanding 3.7
When programming, you _____ statements inside a loop that can change the _____ of the loop.
A. avoid writing, switches
B. avoid writing, conditions
C. usually write, switches
D. usually write, conditions

Programming Challenge 3.3
Update Programming Challenge3.1 so that a user can repeat the practice until exit.

3.2.2 The 'for' Loop

Before learning the 'for' loop, you need to know a type of variable called 'array' that often works with loops. In the last chapter, you learned how to use variables to hold values for calculation or display. One variable can hold only one value at a time. This can be inconvenient. For example, if a class had 10 students, and you wanted to order the scores from high to low, you would need to declare 10 variables, one for each student. An array could make this process much more efficient.

What is an array? An array is just a variable that can hold many values of the same type. Each is differentiated by its index. Let's see an example that uses an array.

Example 3.4

Problem:

A class has 5 students. The school needs an application that can ask the user to enter each student's numeric score for a test, and then display the average, highest score, lowest score, and all five scores from high to low in a row.

Solution:

Start a console app in Visual Studio called Chapter3Example4. With the default Program.cs open in the code view, replace the default code with the following:

```csharp
1    // declare an array that can hold 5 int values
2    int[] scores = new int[5];
3    // using a loop to prompt user for each value
4    for (int i = 0; i<scores.Length; i++)
5    {
6        Console.WriteLine("Enter a core:");
7        scores[i] = int.Parse(Console.ReadLine());
8    }
9    // display the array statistics
10   Console.WriteLine($"Average: {scores.Average():N2}");
11   Console.WriteLine($"Highest: {scores.Max()}");
12   Console.WriteLine($"Lowest: {scores.Min()}");
13   // display all scores from high to low
14   foreach(int s in scores.OrderByDescending(x=>x))
15   {
16       Console.Write(s+" ");
17   }
```

Figure 3.5 Code for Example 3.4

Execute the program. Type in 5 whole numbers, each between 0 and 100. Press the enter after each number. After all 5 scores are entered, you should see the statistics on the console screen. Press enter to end the program.

Explanation:

Line 2 declares an array that can hold 5 int values. Note the difference between declare and initialize a simple type variable and an array:

int score = 90;

int[] scores = new int[5];

The array variable scores holds 5 integers, which are all 0s. The new keyword indicates that this is a reference type. The reference type means that the actual 5 integers are not stored in the array variable 'scores'. Only the memory address of the 5 integers are stored in the variable 'scores'. You will learn more about reference type in Chapter 5 when you learn classes and object-oriented programming.

If you want to initialize an array other than the default value, you can do it like this:

int[] scores = new int[4]{3, 5, 8, 10};

The number "4" in the square bracket is optional.

To access a value in an array, use the indcx. For example, you can print the first value in the above array (which is 3) to the console screen:

Console.WriteLine(scores[0]);

Note the array index starts counting from zero, not one.

Similarly, if you want to change the value of the second score in the array, use the following statement:

scores[1] = 12;

This will change the second value from 5 to 12.

Be very careful of the index value, since they start counting from zero. In the above example, if you use scores[4], you will receive an array out of bound error because there is no element with the index of 4.

Lines 4 to 8 are a loop that repeats the statements between Lines 6 and 7 five times. An int variable "i" is used to control the number of repetitions. Here are the steps for the loop:

Step 1. i = 0

Step 2. Check to see if this is true: i < scores.Length; if true, continue to Step 3. If false, exit the loop. The Length property of an array holds the number of elements in the array (Line 4).

Step 3. Execute the statements in the block enclosed with braces. In this case, Lines 6 and 7 are executed.

Step 4. The i++ statement increases the value in i by 1.

Step 5. Go back to Step 2 above.

This process will continue until the condition in Step 2 is no longer true.

Lines 10 to 12 utilize the built-in methods of arrays (Average(), Max(), Min()) to print the statistics.

Lines 14 to 17 apply the foreach loop. It is sometimes called shorthand for loop. The foreach loop gives out one element at a time from an array without using additional code to arrange the index. An array has a built-in OrderByDescending() method which requires a lambda expression (x=>x) as input. We will discuss more about lambda expression later in this book and our advanced agile book. Line 16 prints with Write(), not WriteLine() method. The former does not include a line break so that all values are displayed in a row. The code also adds a blank space after each value.

Test Your Understanding 3.8
Which of the following statements is true?
1) When you know how many repeating loops you need in the code, the 'for' loop is a good choice.
2) When you don't know how many repeating loops you need in the code, the 'while' loop is a good choice.
A. Only 1) is true
B. Only 2) is true
C. Both 1) and 2) are true
D. Neither 1) nor 2) is true

Test Your Understanding 3.9
A(n) _____ is a variable that can hold many values of the same type. Each is differentiated by its index.
A. super variable
B. multi-value variable
C. global variable
D. array

Test Your Understanding 3.10
What can be stored in the following variable "scores"?
int[] scores;
A. the memory address of an int array.
B. the memory address of an array.
C. a group of 5 int values.
D. an int array.

Test Your Understanding 3.11
What does a reference type of variable do?
A. hold an integer value only
B. hold a floating-point value only
C. hold a string value only
D. hold memory address only

Test Your Understanding 3.12
Given the following statement about a C# array:
int[] scores = new int[4]{3, 5, 8, 10};
What will be printed on the console screen with the following statement?
Console.WriteLine(scores[3]);
A. 3
B. 5
C. 8
D. 10

Test Your Understanding 3.13
Given the following statement about a C# array:
int[] scores = new int[4]{3, 5, 8, 10};
What will be printed on the console screen with the following statement?
Console.WriteLine(scores[4]);
A. 3
B. 4
C. 5
D. Out of bound error.

Programming Challenge 3.4
Write an application that can ask the user for the inches of rainfall for each month in a year. Then the application will display the average, highest, and lowest inches of rainfall for the year. It should also display all 12 rainfall from high to low in a row.

Example 3.5

Problem:
A class has 6 students. The school needs an application that can ask the user to enter each student's numeric test score and then display the number of As (score between 90 and 100 inclusive), number of Bs (score between 80 and 89), number of Cs (score between 70 and 79), number of Ds (score between 60 and 69), and number of Fs (score under 60). The app then displays the average, highest, and lowest numeric scores. It should also display all numeric scores from low to high in a row.

Solution:

Start a console app project in Visual Studio called Chapter3Example5. With the default Program.cs open in the code view window, replace the default code with the following:

```csharp
// create an int array that can hold 6 student scores
int[] scores = new int[6];
// using a loop to prompt user for scores, one at a time
for (int count = 0; count < scores.Length; count++)
{
    Console.WriteLine("Enter a score:");
    scores[count] = int.Parse(Console.ReadLine()!);
}
// variables to hold number of As, Bs, Cs, Ds, and Fs
int numberOfA = 0;
int numberOfB = 0;
int numberOfC = 0;
int numberOfD = 0;
int numberOfF = 0;
// using a loop to check each score to find letter grade
for (int count = 0; count < scores.Length; count++)
{
    if (scores[count] >= 90)
        numberOfA++;
    else if (scores[count] >= 80)
        numberOfB++;
    else if (scores[count] >= 70)
        numberOfC++;
    else if (scores[count] >= 60)
        numberOfD++;
    else
        numberOfF++;
}
// Display the result
Console.WriteLine($"Number of As: {numberOfA}");
Console.WriteLine($"Number of Bs: {numberOfB}");
Console.WriteLine($"Number of Cs: {numberOfC}");
Console.WriteLine($"Number of Ds: {numberOfD}");
Console.WriteLine($"Number of Fs: {numberOfF}");
Console.WriteLine($"Average: {scores.Average():N2}");
Console.WriteLine($"Highest: {scores.Max()}");
Console.WriteLine($"Lowest: {scores.Min()}");
// display all scores from low to high in a row
foreach(int s in scores.OrderBy(x => x))
{
    Console.Write(s + " ");
}
```

Programming Challenge 3.5

Body Mass Index (BMI) is used to determine weight status.

BMI value	Weight Status
Below 18.5 (<18.5)	Underweight
Between 18.5 and 25 (>=18.5 and < 25)	Normal Weight

| Between 25 and 30 (>=25 and < 30) | Overweight |
| 30 or more (>=30) | Obese |

A class has 6 students. The school needs an application that can let the user enter each student's BMI and display the number of students in each weight status, class average BMI value, highest, and lowest weights. The app should also display all weights from low to high in a row.

3.3 Logical Operators

Logical operators evaluate two Boolean expressions (except for the NOT operator) and return with true or false. In this section, you will learn these operators: AND, OR, and NOT.

The AND operator, represented by &&, only returns true when both operands are true. The OR operator, represented by | |, returns true when at least one of the operands is true. Unlike the AND and OR operators, which work on two operands, the NOT operator has a single operand. The NOT operator, represented by !, returns true when the operand is false and returns false when the operand is true.

Example 3.6

Problem:
Modify Example 3.3 so that it will prompt the user for a score and display the message based on the score. The application can repeat the prompt and display the message until the user enters a negative score or a score above 100. The difference from Example 3.3 is that, in this problem, the message is only displayed when the score is in the range of 0 to 100.

Solution:
Open Chapter3Example3 in Visual Studio. Change Line 6 of Figure 3.4 (shown below)

```
while(score >= 0)
```

to

```
while(score >= 0 && score <= 100 )
```

&& is a logical AND operator, which requires both the (score >= 0) and (score <= 100) operands to be true to execute the statements in the block.

Test Your Understanding 3.14

Which of the following statements about logical operators is correct?
1) Logical operators such as &&, ||, and ! can only be used in the conditional expression in the repeating statement, such as 'while'.
2) Logical operators allow the application to handle more complex conditional statements.
A. 1) only
B. 2) only
C. Both 1) and 2)
D. Neither 1) nor 2)

Test Your Understanding 3.15
What is the value of the following logical expression?
(5>3) && (3>5)
A. True
B. False
C. 2
D. -2

Test Your Understanding 3.16
What is the value of the following logical expression?
(5>3) || (3>5)
A. True
B. False
C. 2
D. -2

Test Your Understanding 3.17
What is the value of the following logical expression?
!(5>3)
A. True.
B. False.
C. 2
D. -2

Test Your Understanding 3.18
What is the correct way to test if x is 3 or 4?
A. x = 3 || 4
B. x == 3 || 4
C. x = 3 || x = 4
D. x == 3 || x == 4

Programming Challenge 3.6
Write an application that can display a horizontal bar chart.

The application should prompt the user to enter a whole number between 1 and 50. Then the application will display that number of asterisks on the console screen. For example, if the user enters 9, it will display *********.

The application should continue to prompt the user for a whole number and display that number of asterisks, only terminating when a zero, negative number, or a number larger than 50 is entered. Hint: If you want seven asterisks, just repeat the following line 7 times, Console.Write("*");

Programing Challenge 3.7
Write an application that will display whole numbers from 1 to 30 consecutively in 30 lines. If a number is divisible by 2, display "TT" instead of the number. If a number is divisible by 3, display "TTT" instead of the number. If a number is divisible by both 2 and 3, display "TTTTT" instead of the number. The first 11 lines will look like this:

```
1
TT
TTT
TT
5
TTTTT
7
TT
TTT
TT
11
```

Programming Challenge 3.8
Smith's Fast Food sells burgers, fries, and drinks only. The price of a burger is $1.50. The price of a serving of French fries is $1.20. A cup of drink is $1.00. A combo (one item of each) will receive $.70 discount. There is a limit of one discount per order. Write a program that asks the user for number of items for each food, then displays the total cost, discount if any, and total cost after discount (Assuming no sales tax.). Remember to use const for the unit price of each food.
Hint: the discount limit makes the coding easier. Customers receive a $.70 discount as long as they have at least one burger, one serving of fries, and one cup of drink.

Figure 3.6 Programming Challenge 3.8 sample output with no discount.

```
Microsoft Visual Studio Debug Console
How many burgers would you like?
1
How many servings of fries would you like?
1
How many cups of drink would you like?
2
The total cost: $4.70
Discount: $0.70
Total cost after discount: $4.00
```

Figure 3.7 Programming Challenge 3.8 sample output with one combo discount.

```
Microsoft Visual Studio Debug Console
How many burgers would you like?
2
How many servings of fries would you like?
2
How many cups of drink would you like?
2
The total cost: $7.40
Discount: $0.70
Total cost after discount: $6.70
```

Figure 3.8 Programming Challenge 3.8 sample output with limit of one combo discount.

3.4 Agile Roles

You learned in Chapter One that the Agile Manifesto values individuals and interaction more than the process and tools. You also learned that agile blurs the lines between different roles in the traditional development team (ex. - programmers can also be involved in design, analysis, and testing). However, agile does have three distinct roles. This section will describe these three roles: product owner, scrum master, and team members.

3.4.1 Product Owner

As you learned in Chapter One, one major issue of the Waterfall approach was the lack of user involvement. The product owner fills part of this gap. A product owner is typically a business manager who works on the development team. The product owner may not know much about programming or testing, but she plays the critical role of gathering business requirements for the development team.

The product owner owns the software and can represent the customers who are paying for the project. The product owner must work with the scrum team on a daily basis. When a team member has a question about the requirements, he or she can just ask the product owner without having to leave the room. This enhances communication between the developer and the business.

The product owner's primary jobs are writing up the requirements (called user stories; will be discussed in Chapter 5) with the scrum master (discussed later in this chapter) and prioritizing the requirements with other business managers according to the business values the user story provides.

It is important to note that the product owner is not just a business user. The product owner is the champion or sponsor of the project and has the authority to make decisions for the project, particularly decisions regarding whether a feature is done and can be released (Pichler, 2010).

The product owner is usually a single person, not a committee, so the time it takes to reach an agreement is reduced.

The product owner plays a critical role in the success of the project. He or she directs the product vision and goals and decides what the business values are. There are six characteristics of a good product owner (Pham and Pham. 2012; the authors listed seven, but we think the last characteristic belongs to the scrum master):

1. Deep knowledge of the product being developed.
2. Good at meeting stakeholder's expectations, even with conflicting priorities.
3. Able to gather requirements that achieve the product vision and goals.
4. Be fully available to actively engage with the team at all times.
5. A good organizer who can handle issues on both business and technological sides.
6. A good communicator who can express the requirements from the business to the development team effectively and send frequent feedback to the development team.

Test Your Understanding 3.19
How many product owners are in a typical agile team?
A. 1
B. 2
C. 3
D. 4

Test Your Understanding 3.20
Which of the following statements about the product owner is correct?
1) The product owner must be a good programmer at minimum.
2)The product owner is critical to the success of the development team, but does not write a single line of code.
A. 1) only
B. 2) only
C. Both 1) and 2)
D. Neither 1) nor 2)

Test Your Understanding 3.21
Which of the following is a characteristic of a good product owner?
A. Leadership skills
B. A skilled programmer
C. Deep knowledge of the product being developed
D. Be available to actively engage with the team at least once a day

Test Your Understanding 3.22
Which of the following is a characteristic of a good product owner?
A. Good project manager
B. Deep knowledge of programming language being used
C. Good organizer who can handle business issues
D. Good communicator between the business and the team

3.4.2 Scrum Master

The scrum master has two major responsibilities. One is to ensure team productivity and the other is to monitor project progress by facilitating all scrum meetings and communicating between the team and the business (Resnick et al., 2011, Viscardi, 2013).

To ensure team productivity, the scrum master works as a facilitator and motivator of the development team (Jongerius, et al., 2014). He or she ensures that the team functions as smoothly as possible, whether that is making sure meetings are on time, or that a sick team member is accounted for. Scrum masters should try their best to keep team morale high and remove any obstacles. If the music from next door is too loud, or too many external meetings are requested from the company, the scrum master will be responsible for talking to the people next door, or communicating with the company manager. Because the scrum master manages the team by servicing them, they are often referred to as the "servant leader" (Liden et al., 2014).

To monitor the project's progress, the scrum master facilitates all meetings, such as daily scrum meetings, which function to uncover issues and make adjustments to overcome those issues. He or she makes sure that everyone knows what the goal is, is kept up to date on the progress of the project, and collaborates to achieve that goal. Additionally, the scrum master often decides team size. A scrum master may prefer fewer members if they believe additional members will not increase productivity. The scrum master also acts as a liaison between the team and the clients. Even though the product owner can communicate directly with the development team, the scrum master is usually the first to learn of any major changes from the business side (ex. - major feature changes, budget cuts).

The scrum master also educates and coaches the team on agile (Measey and Radtac, 2015). This includes visualizing team goals and championing the implementation of new technical practices. The team buy-in to the agile approach is critical to success.

Finally, the scrum master makes sure that the team follows agile principles effectively (Cooke, 2010). This includes, but is not limited to, accounting for meeting attendance and ensuring that only the high priority items from the product backlog are selected for the sprint backlog.

Test Your Understanding 3.23

The scrum master is like a project _____ for the team.
A. leader
B. manager
C. facilitator
D. partner

Test Your Understanding 3.24
Servant leader is a term used to describe the _____.

A. product owner
B. scrum master
C. team members
D. none of the above

Test Your Understanding 3.25
What are the two major responsibilities of a scrum master?
A. to ensure team productivity and manage the project
B. to ensure team productivity and monitor project progress
C. to monitor project progress and manage the project
D. to manage the project and help the team in any technical problems

Test Your Understanding 3.26
In an agile team, who serves as a communicator between the business and the development team?
A. scrum master
B. product owner
C. both scrum master and product owner
D. neither scrum master nor product owner

3.4.3 Team Members

Team members are people who actually develop software. How they work determines the quality, scope, budget and schedule of the project. The first step towards teamwork is ensuring trust and transparency between members. This is typically stated in the team working agreement (Payton, 2015).

The agreement should be created via a discussion between team members and the scrum master. The objective is to have a positive and productive experience. The agreement should be written and posted in an easy to see place. It will serve as reference throughout the project.

Team size is typically around five to nine people. This magic range may have originated from a classic publication by Miller (1956) describing limits to how much information human beings can keep in working memory. This range was accepted by the Scrum Guide (2016). Too many members may make collaboration difficult, while too few members can create gaps in skill sets necessary to deliver the software. Do note that there have been cases where three- or four-member teams are successful.

There are five characteristics that an agile team member should have (Cooke, 2012):

1. Multi-skilled: An agile team blurs the lines between traditional roles. Every member needs to be comfortable working in roles they are not used to.

2. Open-minded and flexible: This characteristic ensures that members are not only able to do work outside their expertise, but are willing to do it.

3. Highly communicative: Interactivity is one of the four values stated in the Agile Manifesto. Idea sharing, pair programming, and collaboration all require excellent communication skills.

4. Self-motivated: A self-motivated person can work both as a team player as well as an individual. Agile encourages individual members to decide how he/she wants to work, and what to work on beyond what is assigned by the manager.

5. Holistic thinker: A member in an agile team should be able to appreciate both the technical and business contexts of the product.

Agile methodology favors a set up where all team members are physically located in the same place, as explained in Chapter 2. Then, is it possible for a virtual team to succeed? The answer is yes, as long as team dynamic and collaboration can be established (Crowder and Friess, 2015). Ideally, the team will meet at the beginning of the project and regularly during the project as budget permits.

Test Your Understanding 3.27
For a virtual agile team to succeed, the team must establish _____.
A. team dynamic
B. collaboration
C. both A and B
D none of above

Test Your Understanding 3.28
Agile team members have _____, e.g. analysis, coding.
A. different working hours
B. different responsibilities
C. different goals
D. same responsibilities

Test Your Understanding 3.29

Which of the following is NOT a characteristic of an agile team member?
A. Multi-skilled
B. Highly communicative
C. Self-motivated
D. Atomistic thinker

Test Your Understanding 3.30
Which of the following is NOT an agile role?
A. Project manager
B. Product owner
C. Scrum master
D. Team members

Test Your Understanding 3.31
The normal size for an agile team is _____ people.
A. three to five
B. five to nine
C. nine to eleven
D. more than eleven

Test Your Understanding 3.32
The _____ is the person who makes sure that the team follows the agile principles effectively.
A. product owner
B. scrum master
C. team member
D. product owner and scrum master

3.5 Chapter Summary

In the C# sections of this chapter, you learned how to selectively execute a block of statements based on certain conditions. You also learned how to repeat a block of statements either a pre-defined number of times or as long as certain conditions are true. You can solve most problems with just these three constructions: sequence, conditional, and repetition. You will use these constructions for the rest of the book.

In the agile sections of this chapter, you learned the three roles of agile: product owner, scrum master, and team members. These distinct roles work in collaboration toward the project objectives.

3.6 References

Cooke, J. L. (2010). Agile Principles Unleashed : Proven Approaches for Achieving Real Productivity in Any Organisation. Ely: IT Governance Publishing. Cambridgeshire, UK

Cooke, J. L. , 2012, Everything You Want to Know About Agile: How to Get Agile Results in a Less-Than-Agile Organization. Ely: IT Governance Publishing. Cambridgeshire, UK

Crowder, J. A and Friess, S. 2015, Agile Project Management: Managing for Success, Springer.

Jongerius, P., Offermans, A., Vanhouche, A. Sanwikarja, P., and Geel, J.V. 2014, Get Agile: Scrum for UX, design and development, BIS Publishers, Amsterdam.

Liden, R. C., Wayne, S. J., Liao, C., and Meuser, J. D. 2014, Servant Leadership and Serving Culture: Influence on Individual and Unit Performance, Academy of Management Journal, Oct, 57:5, p 1434-1452.

Measey, P. and Radtac, 2015, Agile Foundations -- Principles, Practices and Frameworks, BCS, Swindon, UK.

Miller, G. A. 1956, The Magic Number Seven, Plus or Minus Two: Some Limits on Our Capacity for Processing Information, Psychological Review, 63, p. 81-97.

Payton, T. 2015, How to create agile team working agreement, Visited November 19, 2016, https://www.scrumalliance.org/community/articles/2015/march/how-to-create-agile-team-working-agreements

Pham, A. and Pham, P. 2012, Scrum in Action: Agile Software Project Management and Development, Course PTR, Boston, MA.

Pichler, Roman. 2010. Agile product management with Scrum: Creating products that customers love. Boston: Addison-Wesley.

Resnick, S., De la Maza, M., Bjork, A., 2011, Professional Scrum with Team Foundation Server 2010, Wrong Guides Series, Wrox, Indianapolis, IN.

Schwaber, K. and Sutherland, J. 2016, The Scrum Guide, available at www.scrumguides.org Visited November 19, 2016.

Viscardi, S. 2013, The Professional ScrumMaster's Handbook: A Collection of Tips, Tricks, and War Stories to Help THE Professional ScrumMaster Break the Chains of Traditional Organization and Management, Packt Publishing, Birmingham, U.K.

3.7 Solutions to Programming Challenges

Programming Challenge 3.1

```csharp
// prompt user for first integer
Console.WriteLine("Enter first integer: ");
// store the integer in a variable
int firstInteger = int.Parse(Console.ReadLine());
// prompt user for second integer
Console.WriteLine("Enter second integer: ");
// store the integer in a variable
int secondInteger = int.Parse(Console.ReadLine());
// display menu
Console.WriteLine("Enter 1, 2, or 3");
Console.WriteLine("1. Addition");
Console.WriteLine("2. Multiplication");
Console.WriteLine("3. Exit");
int selection = int.Parse(Console.ReadLine());
// if 1 is entered
if (selection == 1)
{
    Console.WriteLine(firstInteger + secondInteger);
}
else if (selection == 2)
{
    Console.WriteLine(firstInteger * secondInteger);
}
```

3.8 Solutions to Test Your Understanding

3.1 B; 3.2 C; 3.3 C; 3.4 B; 3.5 B; 3.6 C; 3.7 D; 3.8 C; 3.9 D; 3.10 A; 3.11 D; 3.12 D; 3.13 D; 3.14 B; 3.15 B; 3.16 A; 3.17 B; 3.18 D; 3.19 A; 3.20 B; 3.21 C; 3.22 D; 3.23 C; 3.24 B; 3.25 B; 3.26 C; 3.27 C; 3.28 D; 3.29 D; 3.30 A; 3.31 B; 3.32 B;

Chapter 4: C# Methods and Agile Events

Chapter Learning Outcomes

4.1 Recognizing a method in C# as a logical group of statements
4.2 Exemplifying method usage with method call
4.3 Implementing methods with parameters and return
4.4 Recalling types of events in agile
4.5 Summarizing different types of agile events

4.1 A Method is a Logical Group of Statements

When you give instructions to computers, you write statements by following C# syntax. Applications often have thousands of lines of statements, if not millions. You need a better way to organize these statements. One way is by grouping them into methods.

Statements that accomplish the same task can be grouped into a method. Suppose you would like every line of message displayed in the console to have a blank line before and after the text, with a line of asterisks to separate the messages. You can code this with or without utilizing a method, as we will demonstrate in the next two examples.

Example 4.1

Problem:
Write an application to display the line of text: "C# is fun." Insert a blank line before and after the text and add a line of asterisks after the second blank line.

```
C# is fun.

**********
```

Figure 4.1 Sample output of Chapter4 Example 1.

Solution:

Create a console app project called Chapter4Example1. Replace the default code with the following:

```
Console.WriteLine();
Console.WriteLine("C# is fun.");
Console.WriteLine();
Console.WriteLine("**********");
```

Example 4.2

Problem:

Write an application to display the line of text: "C# is fun." Insert a blank line before and after the text and add a line of asterisks after the second blank line. This time, use a method.

Solution:

Create a console app called Chapter4Example2. Replace the default code with the following:

```
1    class Program
2    {
         0 references
3        static void Main()
4        {
5            DisplayText();
6        }
         1 reference
7        static void DisplayText()
8        {
9            Console.WriteLine();
10           Console.WriteLine("C# is fun.");
11           Console.WriteLine();
12           Console.WriteLine("**********");
13       }
14   }
```

Figure 4.2 Code for Example 4.2

Explanation:

Lines 1, 2, and 14 create a class called Program. A class is a container that can have one or more methods in it. In this example, the Program class has two methods in it.

Lines 3 to 6 define a method called Main. The Main method is the entry point for every C# application. When a program runs, it will start from the statements inside the Main method. In the first three chapters, you don't see a Main method. The statements you wrote are called top-level statements. The Main method is automatically generated by the compiler and contains all top-level statements. From now on, we will explicitly write the Main method. The static modifier is necessary so that there will be only one Main method for a class.

Lines 7 to 13 define a method named DisplayText(). The keyword, static, is a modifier. It makes the DisplayText method static. Not all methods have to be static; this method has to be static because it will be used in the Main method, which is static. The rule is that a static method, such as the Main method, can only call other static methods, such as the DisplayText method.

On Lines 3 and 7, void is a keyword for the return type. In this example, the methods do not return anything, so 'void' is used. DisplayText is the method name. You can name your own method anything you'd like. Just follow the same rules as for naming variables. Conventionally, the first letter of every word in a method name is capitalized (ex. - DisplayStudentName()).This style of function name is called Pascal case.

You cannot skip the ( ) after the method name. It is called the parameter list. A parameter list is used to input any values to be used in the method. In this example, the method does not need anything, so the parameter list is blank. However, the pair of parentheses must still be there.

All statements between Lines 8 and 13 are part of the method body. The method body should be inside a pair of braces {}. These statements are executed to accomplish the goal of the method.

Line 5 inside the Main() method calls the DisplayText() method, which displays the message. One common error for beginners is having a method but never calling the method. The statements inside a method will not be executed automatically except in the Main() method. The method call triggers the statements in the method to be executed. As a result, the sequence of the methods in a class does not matter. Figure 4.3 summarizes the components of a method in C#.

Modifier   Return Type   Method Name   Parameter

```
12          // DisplayText method                          Method
13          static void DisplayText()                      Body
14          {
15              Console.WriteLine();
16              Console.WriteLine("C# is fun.");
17              Console.WriteLine();
18              Console.WriteLine("*********************");
19          }
```

Figure 4.3 Components of a method

Test Your Understanding 4.1
A _____ is a logical group of statements with a common goal.
A. method
B. container
C. logical operator
D. logical object

Test Your Understanding 4.2
Which of the following is NOT a component of a method?
A. method variable
B. method modifier
C. method return type
D. method name

Test Your Understanding 4.3
Which of the following is NOT a component of a method?
A. method modifier
B. method return type
C. method goal
D. parameter list

Test Your Understanding 4.4
What is the parameter in a method?
A. a pair of parentheses
B. value(s) to be used in the method from outside of the method
C. the border of the method
D. an optional value of the method

Test Your Understanding 4.5
What happens if you write a method and do not call it?
A. an error
B. a compiler error
C. statements inside the method will not execute
D. statements inside the method can only execute once

Programming Challenge 4.1
Create a console app with two methods: Main and DisplayMenu. Copy all code from Programming Challenge 3.1 (Section 3.7) and paste them inside the Main method. Next cut the four consecutive lines of Console.WriteLine and paste them inside the DisplayMenu method.

4.2 A Method can have Parameters

You learned in the previous section that a method is a logical group of statements for a common objective. A method can also work on one or more values from outside the method. These values are called parameters of the method.

Example 4.3

Problem:
Modify the Example 4.2 DisplayText() method so that it can display different messages (not just "C# is fun") according to the parameter value passed in from outside.

Analysis:

The original method DisplayText() in Example 4.2 did not get any input (parameter is blank), so it can only display what is written in it. If you allow the method to receive some inputs (arguments), then it will be able to display the inputs. For example, if the user wants to display "Agile is more fun", you don't need to change the method. Just pass the message when calling the method. This is demonstrated in Line 6 of Figure 4.4.

Solution:

Update Example 4.2 so that the Program class looks like Figure 4.4.

```
1     class Program
2     {
          0 references
3         static void Main()
4         {
5             DisplayText("C# is fun!");
6             DisplayText("Agile is more fun!");
7         }
          2 references
8         static void DisplayText(string message)
9         {
10            Console.WriteLine();
11            Console.WriteLine(message);
12            Console.WriteLine();
13            Console.WriteLine("*********");
14        }
15    }
```

Figure 4.4 Code for Example 4.3

Explanation:

Line 8 of Figure 4.4 is different from Line 7 of Figure 4.2. This time, the parameter is no longer blank.

It has a string variable called "message". This means if you want to use/call this method, you have to provide a string value as an argument.

Line 11 in the method body of Figure 4.4 is also different from Line 10 of Figure 4.2. Instead of displaying "C# is fun." on the console screen, it will display any string value passed in by the caller.

Line 5 is calling the DisplayText method. Note that it is different from the method call in the earlier example where you didn't pass an argument to the method. This time, you have to provide a string value, e.g. "C# is fun!"

Line 6 is calling the DisplayText method again with a different argument ("Agile is more fun!"). One benefit of having a method is that you can call it many times.

The value(s) a method expects are often called the parameter(s), and the value(s) passed into the method are often called argument(s). In the example, "message" is a parameter and "Agile is more fun" is an argument.

Test Your Understanding 4.6
The variable(s) that show(s) in the method header is often called a(n) _____.
A. parameter
B. argument
C. agile
D. C#

Test Your Understanding 4.7
The value(s) that is(are) passed to a method is often called a(n) _____.
A. parameter
B. argument
C. agile
D. C#

Test Your Understanding 4.8
A method may accept _____ value(s) to work on.
A. up to one
B. up to two
C. up to three
D. zero or more

Programming Challenge 4.2
Smith's Fast Food sells burgers, fries, and drinks only. The price of a burger is $1.50. The price of a serving of French fries is $1.20. A cup of drink is $1.00. Write a console app with two methods: Main and DisplayPrice. The DisplayPrice method accepts a name of the food (burgers, fries, or drinks) and

returns the corresponding price. The Main method includes the following four lines:

```
DisplayPrice("hamburgers");
DisplayPrice("fries");
DisplayPrice("drinks");
DisplayPrice("lobsters");
```

The output looks like:

```
Microsoft Visual Studio Debug Console
$1.50
$1.20
$1.00
We don't sell that.
```

Figure 4.5 Sample output for Programming Challenge 4.2.

4.3 A Method can Return a Value

So far, your methods do not return anything, as represented by the "void" keyword in the method header. A method often returns a value after the method's work.

Example 4.4

Problem:
Write a method named Plus() that will accept two whole numbers and return the sum of the two values. Demonstrate the Plus() method by calling it from inside the Main() method.

Solution:

```
1    class Program
2    {
         0 references
3        static void Main()
4        {
5            int a = 3;
6            int b = 5;
7            int total = Plus(a,b);
8            Console.WriteLine($"{a} + {b} = {total}");
9        }
         1 reference
10       static int Plus(int a, int b)
11       {
12           int sum;
13           sum = a + b;
14           return sum;
15       }
16   }
```

Figure 4.6 Code for Example 4.4

Explanation:

Line 10 is the header line of the Plus() method. The return type for the Plus() method is not void; it is int. This indicates that the Plus() method will return an int value. The parameter list for this line contains two variables. This means the Plus() method will accept two int values. As a result, this method will accept two input values of int type and return one value of int type.

Line 14 includes a keyword "return", which returns a value that matches the return type declared in the Plus() method header.

Line 7 in the Main() method calls the Plus method. Note it passes two int values because Line 10 requires two int values. The values must match in number and type (int). The sequence also matters.

Test Your Understanding 4.9
Which of the following statements about methods is true?
1) A method must have a "return" keyword inside the method body.
2) A method returned value inside the method body must match the return type in the method header.
A. 1) only
B. 2) only
C. Both 1) and 2)
D. Neither 1) nor 2)

Test Your Understanding 4.10
Which of the following statements about methods is true?
1) A method may return one or many values or references by using multiple return statements.
2) If a method header includes a void keyword, the method should still have a return statement.
A. 1) only
B. 2) only
C. Both 1) and 2)
D. Neither 1) nor 2)

Programming Challenge 4.3

Write a method named Multiply() that will accept two whole numbers and return the multiplication product of the two values. Demonstrate the Multiply() method by calling it from inside the Main() method.

4.4 A Method Can Return More Than One Value

A method can only return one value by using the return statement. If you want a method to return two or more values, you can use the "out" parameter modifier.

Example 4.5

Problem:

Write a method named Divide() that will accept two whole numbers and return the quotient and the remainder of these two values. Demonstrate the Divide() method by calling it from inside the Main() method.

Solution:

Start a new project called Chapter4Example5. Type the code as shown in Figure 4.7.

```
1    class Program
2    {
         0 references
3        static void Main()
4        {
5            int a = 14;
6            int b = 5;
7            int quotient = Divide(a, b, out int remainder);
8            Console.WriteLine($"{a} / {b} = {quotient}R{remainder}");
9        }
         1 reference
10       static int Divide(int x, int y, out int r)
11       {
12           int quotient;
13           quotient = x / y;
14           r = x % y;
15           return quotient;
16       }
17   }
```

Figure 4.7 Code for Example 4.5

Explanation:

Line 7 declares an inline variable called remainder that can hold the remainder value. The method passes more than just the dividend (a) and the divisor (b). It also passes the remainder. Note the remainder has an "out" keyword before the type.

Line 10 defines the Divide() method with 'out' as the parameter modifier.

Line 14 assigns a value to the variable r, which is the remainder.

The out modifier actually modifies the variable value passed into a method. To see the difference between 'out' and 'no out', add this line of code x = x *x; right before Line 15. It won't change the variable 'a' value that is passed into the method since the 'x' variable in Line 10 does not have the 'out' keyword.

Using the "out" parameter modifier allows you to return more than one value back from a method.

Test Your Understanding 4.11
Which of the following statements about methods is correct?
1) The 'out' parameter modifier makes it possible for a method to return more than one value.
2) The 'out' parameter modifier is required only when declaring a method.
A. 1) only
B. 2) only
C. Both 1) and 2)
D. Neither 1) nor 2)

Programming Challenge 4.4
Write a method called SumAndDifference() that will accept two whole numbers and return the sum and the difference of the two values (ex. - if the two input whole numbers were 5 and 2, the sum would be 7 and the difference would be 3). Demonstrate the method by calling it from the Main() method.

Programming Challenge 4.5
Write a method called Square() that will accept a whole number between 1 and 20. The method will print a solid square of asterisks with that number of asterisks on each side. In the main method, prompt the user to enter a whole number between 1 and 20. Then call the method to display a solid square of asterisks. For example, if a user entered 3, the output would look like:
* * *

* * *

* * *

Example 4.6

Problem: Rock Paper Scissors
Develop a console application in C# to allow a user to play Rock-Paper-Scissors against the computer. On the console screen, a player can type Rock, Paper, or Scissors. At the same time, the computer will display one of the three words in random. Then the application will display who is the winner.

Additionally, the application will prompt the user if he or she wants to play again.

Solution:

This example has the most lines of code so far. Divide the code into methods for better organization and comprehension. Build one part at a time. Save and test each part before moving on to the next step.

Step 1: Computer always wins

Start a new project called Chapter4Example6. Type in the code as shown in Figure 4.8.

```
1    class Program
2    {
         0 references
3        static string UserShape()
4        {
5            string str;
6            str = "ROCK";
7            return str;
8        }
         0 references
9        static string ComputerShape()
10       {
11           string str;
12           str = "PAPER";
13           return str;
14       }
         0 references
15       static string Winner(string user, string computer)
16       {
17           string winner = "Nobody";
18           if (user == "ROCK" && computer == "PAPER")
19               winner = "computer";
20           return winner;
21       }
         0 references
22       static void Main()
23       {
24
25       }
26   }
```

Figure 4.8 Code for Chapter4Example6 Step 1 Part 1.

Explanation:

Lines 3 to 8 define the UserShape() method, which always returns "ROCK" for testing purposes. The completed method will be in Step 2.

Lines 9 to 14 define the ComputerShape() method, which always returns "PAPER" for testing purposes. The completed method will be in Step 4.

Lines 15 to 21 define the Winner() method, which has two parameters: user and computer. It returns the winner. It checks only one simple case. A more detailed check will be performed in Step 3.

Lines 22 to 25 define the Main method. Add the code from Figure 4.9 inside the Main method.

```
24              bool playAgain = true;
25              while (playAgain)
26              {
27                  string userShape=UserShape();
28                  string computerShape=ComputerShape();
29                  string winner = Winner(userShape, computerShape);
30                  Console.WriteLine($"User shape: {userShape}");
31                  Console.WriteLine($"Computer shape: {computerShape}");
32                  Console.WriteLine($"The winner is: {winner}");
33                  Console.WriteLine("Play again? y/n");
34                  string choice = Console.ReadLine().ToUpper();
35                  if (choice == "Y" || choice == "YES")
36                      playAgain = true;
37                  else
38                  {
39                      Console.WriteLine("Thanks for playing.");
40                      playAgain=false;
41                  }
42              }
```

Figure 4.9 Code for Chapter4Example6 Step 1 Main method.

Explanation:

Line 24 declares a Boolean variable to control the loop. It initializes a true value so the while loop can

start. Lines 33 to 41 prompt user again for a possible change of the value. A Boolean variable can only

hold two values: true or false. Such variables are good for controlling loops or conditional statements.

Lines 25 to 42 are a loop that allows a user to play as many times as he or she desires.

Line 27 calls the UserShape() method, which is defined in Figure 4.8. It stores the returned value in a

string variable called userShape.

Line 28 calls the ComputerShape() method, which is also defined in Figure 4.8. It stores the returned

value in a string variable called computerShape.

Line 29 calls the Winner() method, which is defined in Figure 4.8. It includes two arguments,

userShape and computerShape, and returns a string. The returned value is stored in a string called

winner.

Lines 30 to 32 display the results of user shape, computer shape, and the winner.

Line 34 uses the ToUpper() method of a string to convert user input to all uppercase (so that user

input will be case insensitive).

Save and run the application. The user always shows ROCK, and the computer always shows PAPER, thus making the computer the guaranteed winner. You can play as many times as desired.

Step 2: Player can choose to draw or lose

Update the UserShape() method with the code below:

```
string str;
str = "ROCK";
bool isCorrectSpelling = false;
while (!isCorrectSpelling)
{
    Console.WriteLine("Enter Rock, Paper, or Scissors:");
    str = Console.ReadLine().ToUpper();
    if (str == "ROCK" || str == "PAPER" || str == "SCISSORS")
        isCorrectSpelling = true;
}
return str;
```

Explanation

A Boolean variable, isCorrectSpelling is used to control the while loop. If the user did not spell ROCK, PAPER, or SCISSORS correctly, the loop would prompt for another input.

The ToUpper() method of a string makes the user input case insensitive.

Save and run the application.

Even though the user can enter any one of the three shapes, the result will either be a loss or a tie: if the user enters ROCK, he or she will lose; if the user enters any other shape, it will be a tie. This is due to our currently incomplete winner checking method.

Step 3: Player can choose to win, lose, or draw

Update the Winner() method with the code below:

```
string winner = "Nobody";
if (user == "ROCK" && computer == "PAPER"
    || user == "PAPER" && computer == "SCISSORS"
    || user == "SCISSORS" && computer == "ROCK")
    winner = "computer";
else if (user == "ROCK" && computer == "SCISSORS"
    || user == "PAPER" && computer == "ROCK"
    || user == "SCISSORS" && computer == "PAPER")
    winner = "Player";
return winner;
```

Explanation

The method checks only if the computer wins or the player wins. Everything else counts as nobody winning (a draw).

Save and run the application. Since the computer still only shows PAPER, you can easily play to win. Try playing, and see if you can get the expected results.

Step 4: It's a real game

Update the ComputerShape() method with the code from Figure 4.10.

```
19            string str;
20            str = "PAPER";
21            Random random = new Random();
22            int randomNumber = random.Next(1, 4);
23            switch (randomNumber)
24            {
25                case 1:
26                    str = "ROCK";
27                    break;
28                case 2:
29                    str = "PAPER";
30                    break;
31                case 3:
32                    str = "SCISSORS";
33                    break;
34            }
35            return str;
```

Figure 4.10 Code for the ComuterShape() method.

Explanation

Line 21 instantiates a Random object called 'random' from the Random class.

Line 22 calls the Next() method of the Random class to generate a random number between 1 (included) and 4 (not included).

Lines 23 to 34 use the switch statement to convert the random number to text describing the shape. You can use an if statement to accomplish this as well.

Save and run the application. Test it multiple times to see if there are any errors.

Programming Challenge 4.6
Modify the Rock-Paper-Scissors game so that a player can choose to play 'best two out of three games' or 'best three out of five games'.

4.5 Agile Events

As you learned in Chapter 2, there are three roles, five events, and three artifacts in Scrum. You learned the three roles in Chapter 3. You will learn the five events in this chapter. Scrum founders want you to use prescribed events to create consistency and to avoid any extra meetings. There are five events defined in the 2017 Scrum Guide (Schwaber and Sutherland, 2017). All scrum events are time-boxed, meaning the duration of the events have been predetermined and agreed upon by all members of the scrum team.

Test Your Understanding 4.12
The purpose of having regular scrum event meetings is to _____.
A. avoid additional meetings
B. control meeting time
C. train new members
D. communicate with customers

Test Your Understanding 4.13
All scrum events are time-boxed, which means _____.
A. all events have the same length
B. all events have their own predetermined length
C. all event lengths are recorded
D. all events can take as much time as they require

4.5.1 The Sprint

In Chapter One, we introduced the concept of sprints when we compared the similarities and differences between waterfall and agile approaches. A sprint is a container event that includes all tasks that are necessary to achieve a delivery. From our toy retailer example, outlined in Chapter 1, a sprint might include the events for the development of features that allow the owner to check inventory levels and add new arrivals. At the end of the sprint, the development team will deliver the components of the application that allow the owner to check inventory and update inventory when new shipments arrive. Such a delivery is called an increment.

A sprint starts with sprint planning. Then, on a daily basis, the team should have brief scrum meetings. And, of course, sprints involve the actual work of completing the delivery. At the end of the sprint, the team should have a sprint review and sprint retrospective. Later in the chapter, you will learn each of these events in more detail.

A sprint duration is typically two weeks, but can be as long as a month. The purpose of limiting the duration is to increase the predictability of the software. During this short sprint, the delivery scope is less likely to be changed, and the risk of abandoning the delivery is lower.

The sprint duration should be the same for all sprints in the project. The length is agreed upon at the beginning of the project between the product owner, scrum master, and the scrum team. On rare occasions, a sprint duration may be longer in order to complete a delivery (e.g. when the delivery cannot fit into a sprint).

A sprint can be canceled if the goal of the delivery is no longer valid. In our toy retailer example, if you have a sprint working on a shopping cart software, and the owner decided to purchase the shopping cart software, then there's no longer a reason to continue the sprint. The product owner decides whether to cancel or not. When a sprint is canceled, any completed items are reviewed and may be released if the product owner desires so.

There are basic rules to sprints. During the sprint, changes are not allowed to user stories already in the sprint. If the product owner wants to make any changes, he or she can update the product backlog (a concept that will be explained in the next chapter), which contains all the user stories. This allows the team to focus on the current task.

During the sprint, the development team is not allowed to lower the quality of the goal either. This is to protect the benefits of the customer. However, as the product owner and the development team learn more about the product, a sprint clarification of the scope is allowed.

Test Your Understanding 4.14
Which of the following statements about agile sprint is correct?
1) A sprint delivers a software increment.
2) Shorter sprints make the delivery scope less likely to be changed.
A. 1) only
B. 2) only
C. Both 1) and 2)
D. Neither 1) nor 2)

Test Your Understanding 4.15
Which of the following statements about agile sprint is correct?
1) The length of a sprint is always determined by the user story. The longer the story, the longer the sprint.
2) The product owner is the only person allowed to make changes to stories already in a sprint.
A. 1) only
B. 2) only
C. Both 1) and 2)
D. Neither 1) nor 2)

Test Your Understanding 4.16
Which of the following is NOT a sprint event?
A. sprint planning
B. daily scrum meeting
C. sprint review
D. scrum master

Test Your Understanding 4.17
Which of the following statements about agile is correct?
1) An agile team can slightly lower the quality of the product in order to meet the sprint deadline.
2) A product owner can make changes to the user stories in the product backlog.
A. 1) only
B. 2) only
C. Both 1) and 2)
D. Neither 1) nor 2)

4.5.2 Sprint Planning

A sprint starts with a plan meeting. The main purpose of the meeting is to pick stories from the product backlog that can be completed in one sprint (Sutherland, 2014). There are three agenda items to a sprint plan meeting:

1. Which user stories should be included in this sprint? This is determined by the priority list of the user stories in the product backlog and the projected capacity of the team for the sprint. To accomplish this task, all team members should have a thorough understanding of the user stories in the product backlog. Every story in the product backlog has a priority ranking (set by the product owner) and story points (estimated by the team members). The story points for a story indicate how much effort is needed. The team picks stories by ranking them from high to low. How many stories they pick is based on how many story points the team can complete in one sprint. The total story points selected should not be greater than that the team can complete in one sprint. Deviating slightly in terms of priority ranking and total story points is allowed.

2. After the stories are picked, it is time to write the sprint goal. The sprint goal explains the reasons for the work and provides motivation for running the sprint. A sprint goal must be specific, measurable, and attainable (Pichler, 2012). In our toy retailer example, the sprint goal could be "Mr. Lincoln can update the inventory when a new shipment arrives".

3. The development team decides how to achieve the goal and successfully deliver the software increment in this order: first, the user stories will be broken down into more manageable individual tasks. Next, each member picks the tasks he or she is comfortable completing. Lastly, each member reports an estimate of when he or she will finish. This estimate is usually measured in hours.

Three items above are collectively called the sprint backlog.

A sprint planning meeting is suggested to last 8 hours for a month-long sprint. Shorter sprints should correspond with shorter time-boxes.

Test Your Understanding 4.18
Which of the following is NOT an agenda item on a sprint planning meeting?

A. take attendance
B. pick stories from product backlog
C. write sprint goal
D. decide how to achieve the goal

Test Your Understanding 4.19
Suppose there are five stories in the product backlog:
Story 1: 20 points
Story 2: 40 points
Story 3: 40 points
Story 4: 13 points
Story 5: 20 points
If the team can complete 70 story points per sprint (their 'velocity'), and the priority is the same as the story number (meaning 1 is of highest priority, and 5 the lowest), which stories will probably be picked by the team?
A. Story 1, Story 3, and Story 5
B. Story 1, Story 2, and Story 4
C. Story 2, Story 4, and Story 5
D. Story 1, Story 3, and Story 4

4.5.3 Daily Scrum

Daily scrum is a meeting amongst the development team, time-boxed at 15 minutes. To avoid long meetings, members are required to stand up. Every member answers the following three questions.

1. What did I do yesterday?

2. What will I do today?

3. Do I see any impediments for me or the team?

Daily scrum meetings are not simple status updates. The daily scrum is a time to make commitments. If a member states he or she will complete the "Add new inventory" feature today, you should expect to see that done by tomorrow's meeting.

Compared to the status update meeting, which is typically held once a week or once a month, daily scrum has the advantage of identifying problems early (Hoogendoorn, 2014). Members may delay reporting problems or issues due to laziness or shyness if they only meet once a month. With daily scrum, slow progress is immediately visible.

The meeting also helps members know what others are doing. It can show who needs help. It also provides transparency.

The scrum master should help resolve any issues raised by a member. If a member does not know how to make something work, the scrum master helps.

Test Your Understanding 4.20
Daily scrum meetings should have members standing to _____.
A. make it formal
B. avoid prolonging the meeting
C. keep members healthy
D. facilitate communication

Test Your Understanding 4.21
Which of the following questions is NOT asked in the daily scrum meeting?
A. What did I do yesterday?
B. What will I do today?
C. What do I plan to do tomorrow?
D. Do I see any impediments for me or the team?

4.5.4 Sprint Review Meeting

At the end of the sprint, the team meets to inspect the increment, usually accompanied by a live software demo to show to the business users. The meeting will also update the product backlog according to feedback.

The meeting is time-boxed at four hours for a month-long sprint. The meeting is informal, and any stakeholder can attend. The key value is to get feedback from the business users. To enforce the informality, some teams forbid the use of PowerPoint slides.

The key purpose is to compare the completed increment with the sprint goal set up from the sprint planning meeting, and to see how close the goal is to being achieved.

The review can be a bit daunting, since it is one of few events where multiple stakeholders are directly involved. Stakeholders may ask questions the team is not prepared for. Features may not work as planned. However, team members should remember that this is not a status check. The purpose of the review is to elicit feedback and nurture collaboration.

There are four keys to the success of a sprint review (Lacey, 2016).

1. Take time to plan. Planning can increase the team's confidence. Take time to set up the software so that customers can interact with the product.

2. Document decisions. People tend to forget things. Keeping track of customer statements in print makes everyone accountable.

3. Ask for acceptance. Customers may or may not accept the product on the spot at the review meeting. It never hurts to ask, particularly for what can be improved. It is important that the team meet the "definition of done" in the first place.

4. Be brave. The review meeting can be intimidating, since the customer may not accept the increment. Members may panic. The team should try their best to communicate with the customers and work closely with the product owner to reach their goal.

Test Your Understanding 4.22
Which of the following is NOT a key to success in a sprint review meeting?
A. Take time to plan
B. Document decisions
C. Ask for acceptance
D. Make it a formal meeting with customers

Test Your Understanding 4.23
Which of the following is NOT a purpose of the sprint review?
A. Customers can check the status of the project.
B. The team can check how close they are to the sprint goal.
C. The team elicits feedback from the customers.
D. The team and the customers get to collaborate.

4.5.5 Sprint Retrospective

Sprint retrospective is a three-hour meeting for a one-month long sprint. It is held after the sprint review meeting and before the new sprint. All members, including the scrum master and the product owner, should attend the meeting. It has three purposes:

1. To examine how well the last sprint went.
2. To list what went well and what did not go well.
3. To plan for improvement.

There are many ways to achieve the three purposes (Cohn, 2010). One way is to let every member in the team voice what should be implemented in the next sprint, what should be continued in the next sprint, and what should be stopped. After a list is made, the team votes. Based on the results and possibly further discussion, a plan for the next sprint is created.

Retrospectives are often omitted by scrum teams that believe the meetings are optional and don't directly add value to the product (Lacey, 2016). This omission is often the beginning of a failed scrum practice. Recall the three foundations of scrum you learned in Chapter 2: transparency, inspection, and adaptation. All other events discussed in this section focus on the product delivery. This is the only event that can support all three foundations. This meeting helps team members know how to work more efficiently and productively. This is also the only time the team learns about new techniques in the field that they can utilize.

There are four keys to the success of a sprint retrospective (Lacey, 2016).

1. Show them the way: The retrospective schedule should be brief enough to avoid schedule conflicts. Right before the meeting, a reminder should be sent out that includes the meeting agenda, the benefits of the meeting, and how to prepare for the meeting.

2. Build a good environment: One major problem with the retrospective meeting is the endless discussion on one issue and inability to reach an agreement. You can either remove chairs and/or use a timer for each agenda item to limit the discussion. In addition, make necessary artifacts available so that the team can inspect and adapt. These items include "burn-down" charts (which indicate how many stories are left in the backlog; agile metrics will be discussed in Chapter 6) and the team's vision for the product and sprint (sprint artifacts will be discussed in detail in the next chapter).

Even though members should trust each other and are allowed to work with a lot of freedom, some ground rules will help. These rules should be made available to all participants before the meeting. Example rules include being respectful, putting away laptops/phones, and not interrupting while others speak.

3. Hold them when you need them: Retrospectives are not just held at the end of a sprint. It can be held anytime a big issue arises, like if there is a major defect, or a change in team membership. It can also be held after a major release, or when the customers demand one. This is analogous to a time out in a basketball game.

4. Set high priority: You should not hold a retrospective only when there's a problem for the team. It is good for supporting scrum foundations and team self-organization. Many beginner agile teams realize this too late.

Test Your Understanding 4.24
The sprint _____ meeting is a time when the team can see what they did well and what needs improvement from the past sprint.
A. daily scrum
B. retrospective
C. review
D. improvement

Test Your Understanding 4.25
Which of the following is NOT a purpose of sprint retrospectives?
A. Examining how well the last sprint went.
B. Listing what went well and what did not go well.
C. Planning for improvement.
D. To demo the software to the customers.

Test Your Understanding 4.26
Which of the following is NOT a key to the success of a sprint retrospective?
A. Show them the way.
B. Product owner should not be present.
C. Build a good environment.
D. Hold them when you need them.

Test Your Understanding 4.27
When should a team hold a sprint retrospective?
A. After the sprint review.
B. Any time a big issue arises.
C. At the end of the sprint, plus any time a big issue happens.
D. When a new user story is added to the product backlog.

4.6 Chapter Summary

In this chapter, you learned how to organize logically related C# statements into a method. A method can have parameters that receive arguments from the caller. A method can also return a value. A method makes your code better organized. Better-organized code makes maintenance much easier, and thus saves money for the business.

You also learned the five events for scrum. They are the sprint, sprint plan meeting, daily scrum, sprint review meeting, and sprint retrospective. These meetings make the scrum practice more consistent, and prevent additional unnecessary meetings.

4.7 References

Cohn, M. (2010), Succeeding with Agile: Software Development Using Scrum, Addison-Wesley Professional PTG.

Hoogendoorn, S., (2014), This Is Agile, Beyond the Basics, Beyond the Hype, Beyond Scrum, Dymaxicon, Sausalito, CA.

Lacey, M. (2016), The Scrum Field Guide, 2nd Edition, Addison-Wesley, Boston.

Pichler, R., (2012), Effective Sprint Goals, Available at

http://www.romanpichler.com/blog/effective-sprint-goals/ Visited November 20, 2016.

Schwaber, K. and Sutherland, J. (2017), The Scrum Guide, available at www.scrumguides.org Visited November 20, 2018.

Sutherland, J. (2014), Scrum the Art of Doing Twice the Work in Half the Time, Crown Business, New York.

4.8 Solutions to Selected Programming Challenges

Programming Challenge 4.5

```csharp
class Program
{
    static void Main()
    {
        Console.WriteLine("Enter an integer:");
        int m = int.Parse(Console.ReadLine());
        Square(m);
    }
    static void Square(int n)
    {
        if(n > 0 || n <= 20)
        {
            for(int i = 0; i < n; i++)
            {
                for(int j = 0; j < n; j++)
                {
                    Console.Write("* ");
                }
                Console.WriteLine();
            }
        }
    }
}
```

4.9 Solutions to Test Your Understanding

4.1 A; 4.2 A; 4.3 C; 4.4 B; 4.5 C; 4.6 A; 4.7 B; 4.8 D; 4.9 B; 4.10 D; 4.11 A; 4.12 A; 4.13 B; 4.14 C; 4.15 D; 4.16 D; 4.17 B; 4.18 A; 4.19 B; 4.20 B; 4.21 C; 4.22 D; 4.23 A; 4.24 B; 4.25 D; 4.26 B; 4.27 C;

Chapter 5: C# Classes and Agile Artifacts

5.1 A Class is a Logical Group of Methods and Fields

In the last chapter, you learned how to group a block of statements with a common goal into a method. In this chapter, you will learn how to group a set of related methods into a class. Because methods usually need data to work on, a class will also contain the related data. In Object Oriented Programming (OOP) terminology, data is termed 'fields'.

The concept of a class is not new to you. You have used classes in Chapter Four; the class name was Program, and your program class always contains a Main() method. In this chapter, you will learn how to create your own custom class by following the Object-Oriented Programming approach.

A class is a conceptual category, like students, employees, cars, or houses. A class is not an object; an object is a specific instance that belongs to a class. So, if you had the class 'students', 'Alice' may be an object of that class. Or, as another example, a class could be the blueprints to a certain model of house, and the house built from that is the object of that class. When you program the object-oriented way, you create a class. When you need to use an object, you use the class to instantiate an object. In Chapter 4, you declared a random object from the Random class in order to use its Next method.

A class keeps track of a certain status. For example, all students have a name and GPA. Therefore, the student class includes name and GPA as statuses. As another example, all cars have a make and color. The car class would have make and color as statuses. In OOP, the statuses of a class are called 'fields'.

A class also has behaviors. Students can take a course, or convert a numeric grade to a letter grade. A car can speed up or down, or change tires. In OOP, these behaviors are called 'methods'.

In short, a class is a conceptual category. A class can have fields to keep track of statuses and methods to carry out actions. In most cases, you will create an object to use the methods.

Test Your Understanding 5.1
Which of the following statements about C# class is correct?
1) A class is a logical group of methods and fields.
2) In OOP, classes and objects are the same thing.
A. 1) only
B. 2) only
C. Both 1) and 2)
D. Neither 1) nor 2)

Test Your Understanding 5.2
In OOP, a class is like a _____, and an object is like a _____ built out of that _____.
A. house, blueprint, construction materials
B. house, room, construction materials
C. house, room, house
D. blueprint, house, blueprint

Test Your Understanding 5.3
John Doe is a student. In OOP terminology, which of the following statements is correct?
A. John Doe is a class
B. John Doe is an object
C. Student is an object
D. Both John Doe and students are objects

Test Your Understanding 5.4
A class can have _____ to keep track of statuses and _____ to carry out actions.
A. objects, fields
B. fields, methods
C. objects, methods
D. methods, objects

Example 5.1

Problem:

A student has a name and a numerical grade/score. The numerical score can be converted to a letter grade. Create a class called Student with those fields (name and numeric score) and method (change numeric score to letter grade). Then demonstrate the class by instantiating the two student objects shown below.

Name: Lynn, numeric score: 97
Name: Bob, numeric score: 87

Finally, print the two students' names and letter grades on the console screen.

The formula for converting a numeric score to a letter grade is 90-100 A; 80-89 B; 70-79 C; 60-69 D; 0-59 F.

Analysis:

You can easily program this problem with just the default Program class and the Main() method, with all your statements inside the Main() method. However, you should learn how to code in OOP so you can handle more difficult problems as they come along and build more robust applications.

The student class has two fields: student name and student score. These fields will store individual name and numeric score. The student class also has the method GetLetterGrade(), which will return a letter grade based on the student score field value.

Solution:

By following this solution, you will learn how to solve the problem in OOP.
In the problem, you can see that student is a class that has name and score fields, and has a method that converts a numeric score to a letter grade.

Create a console app called Chapter5Example1. In the "Solution Explorer" window, right click on the Chapter5Exampe1 Project (not the solution). In the pop-up context menu, point to "Add" then "Class" in the submenu, as shown in the Figure 5.1.

Figure 5.1 Create a class in a project

The "Add new item" dialog will pop up as shown in Figure 5.2. Type in the new name 'Student.cs' then click on the "Add" button. This will create a new class called Student in the project, as shown in Figure 5.3.

Figure 5.2 Add New Item Dialog window.

Figure 5.3 Class template created by Visual Studio.

You will add all components of the Student class inside the class braces, { and }, between Lines 10 and 11 of Figure 5.3. Move the cursor to Line 10 after the beginning brace {. Push enter a few times and type in the code below:

```csharp
// fields
private string name;
private int score;
// properties
public string Name
{
    get { return name; }
    set { name = value; }
}
public int Score
{
    get { return score; }
    set { score = value; }
}
// constructor(s)
public Student(string name, int score)
{
    this.name = name;
    this.score = score;
}
// method(s)
public char GetLetterGrade()
{
    char letterGrade;
    if (Score >= 90)
        letterGrade = 'A';
    else if (Score >= 80)
        letterGrade = 'B';
    else if (Score >= 70)
        letterGrade = 'C';
    else if (Score >= 60)
        letterGrade = 'D';
    else
        letterGrade = 'F';
    return letterGrade;
}
// ToString
public override string ToString()
{
    string str;
    str = $"Name: {Name} Letter Grade: {GetLetterGrade()}";
    return str;
}
```

Explanation:

The field section declares two private variables called fields: one to store student name, and the other to store student score. The first one should be a string data type, and the second one should be an int data type. The private modifier allows this variable to be used only inside this class. In OOP terminology, this is called encapsulation, which prevents outside objects from accessing the implementation details of a class.

The next section includes two properties. A property provides access to a field, so a property is typically public and related to a specific field. One property for one field. It allows the retrieval of the field value from the field or the storage of a value to the field. The "value" in the code is a keyword. It represents the value assigned to the property. For example: In code outside of this class, you cannot assign a value like this name = "Lynn" because name is private. However, you can do Name = "Lynn" because Name (note the uppercase first letter) is a public property. Inside the class, it is a good practice to avoid using a field directly. The student class has two fields. There are two corresponding properties. Note, by convention, a field name begins with a lower-case letter while a property name begins with a capital letter.

The constructor section can have one or more constructors. A constructor of a class is a special method that is called every time a new object is created. Usually, you use a constructor to initialize the field values. You might have noticed the use of the "this" keyword, which points to the object itself. Since you have two name variables, one in the constructor parameter, the other in the field, the keyword "this" makes the two different. The this.name is the one in the field, and name refers to the one in the parameter. The assignment assigns the value from the parameter to the variable in the field.

A constructor does not have a return type (not even the "void" keyword). A constructor must have the same name as the class, including the case. In this example, both the constructor and the class are called Student.

The method section includes zero or more methods. The GetLetterGrade() method in the Student class checks the student's numeric score and returns a letter grade for the student.

The ToString section has the ToString method. It is a special method that returns a string value of an object. You can modify it so that it returns different values or returns the same values in a different format. Every class has a ToString() method by default inherited from the "Object" class. C# makes all classes automatically inherited from the "Object" class. The keyword "override" simply means that this class won't use the default ToString() method implementation of the Object class and will use this new one. ToString() is very convenient, and you should get used to having one for every class you create. It is a good practice to use properties instead of fields inside the ToString method.

In summary, a class typically has zero or many fields. Each field has a corresponding property. A class also has one or many constructors. Additionally, a class has zero or many methods for class behavior. All classes come with a ToString() method, which you should override to have a meaningful outcome when an object of the class is printed.

Test Your Understanding 5.5
By convention, a field name begins with a(n) _____ case letter while a property name begins with a(n) _____ case letter.
A. lower, upper
B. upper, lower
C. lower, lower
D. upper, upper

Test Your Understanding 5.6
A(n) _____ of a class allows the retrieval of the field value or the storage of a value to the field.
A. property
B. constructor
C. object
D. toString method

Test Your Understanding 5.7
A _____ of a class is a special method that is called every time a new object is created.
A. field
B. property
C. constructor
D. toString method

Test Your Understanding 5.8
In the following code snippet, what is the purpose of using the keyword "this"?
private string name;

```
private int score;
public Student(string name, int score)
{
        this.name = name;
        this.score = score;
}
```
A. this.name refers to the name in the field.
B. name refers to the name in the field.
C. this.name refers to the variable with the same name inside the constructor.
D. this.name is the same as name.

Test Your Understanding 5.9
Which of the following is NOT a component of a class?
A. fields
B. properties
C. methods
D. repeating statements

Next, go to the "Solution Explorer" window and click on the "Program.cs" file to display it in the

code window. Replace the default code with the following:

```
1   namespace Chapter5Example1
2   {
        0 references
3       public class Program
4       {
            0 references
5           static void Main()
6           {
7               // create two student instances
8               Student student1 = new Student("Lynn", 97);
9               Student student2 = new Student("Bob", 87);
10              // display the student data
11              Console.WriteLine(student1);
12              Console.WriteLine(student2);
13          }
14      }
15  }
```

Figure 5.4 The Main() method demonstrates the Student class.

Explanation:

Line 8 creates a student object, called student1, by calling the constructor of the Student class and

passing two arguments, "Lynn" for name and 97 for her score. A Student type variable called student1 is declared and assigned the reference to the newly created Student object.

There are three things that happen here. First, in the heap area of computer memory, an unnamed object with a string value of "Lynn" and an int value of 97 is created. Second, in the stack area of computer memory, a Student type variable called student1 is created. Third, the memory address of that unnamed object is stored in the student1. If skipping the "Third", the student1 will store null. The memory address is often referred to as "reference". For now, just need to know the heap area is the slower area in memory and the stack area is the faster area in memory.

Line 11 prints the object student1. It will automatically call the ToString() method of the Student class. For learning purposes, you are encouraged to make some changes to the ToString() method of the Student class. You can see how the console display changes when you run the program again.

In Figure 5.4, you notice a new term, "namespace". A namespace is a container which starts with the keyword, namespace, followed by a name and a pair of curly braces. A namespace can contain one or more classes. A class is also a container that can have one or more methods. Finally, a method is a container that can have zero or more instructions. All containers have a container header followed by a pair of curly braces. All code for the rest of the book will follow the structure of namespace, class, and method.

Test Your Understanding 5.10
Suppose s1 is an object of the Student class. What will the following statement do?
Console.WriteLine(s1);
A. s1 will be displayed on the console screen.
B. the ToString() method of the Student class will be called.
C. the constructor of the Student class will be called if defined.
D. a compiler error will result if the ToString() method of the Student class is not defined.

Test Your Understanding 5.11
Which of the following statements about class is correct?
1) When creating a new object of a class, a constructor of the class is called.
2) When creating a new object of a class, the object's name is always "new".
A. 1) only.
B. 2) only.
C. Both 1) and 2)
D. Neither 1) nor 2)

Test Your Understanding 5.12
You cannot live in a blueprint. You have to build a house to live in it. Similarly, for most classes, you cannot use it directly, you have to create an _____ of the class before calling its methods.
1) instance
2) object
A. 1) only.
B. 2) only.
C. Both 1) and 2)
D. Neither 1) nor 2)

Programming Challenge 5.1
An employee has a name, a payrate, and an hoursWorked. The pay amount can be calculated by multiplying payrate and hoursWorked. Create a class called Employee with three fields (name, payrate, and hoursWorked). The data type for the name should be a string. The data type for payrate and hoursWorked should be double. The class should have a method called GetPayAmount that returns pay amount. The return data type must be double. The class should also include properties, constructor(s), and the ToString method. The ToString method must display employee name and pay amount. The class must be in its own cs file.
Then, inside the Main method of the Program class, demonstrate the Employee class by instantiating two employee objects with made up data. One of the employees must be you. Next print both employees.

Example 5.2

Problem: Tic Tac Toe

Develop a console application of the Tic Tac Toe game. The Tic Tac Toe board includes nine squares in three rows by three columns. The game starts with all empty squares each marked with an "E". Two players take turns declaring squares. Whoever claims three consecutive squares first wins. The first player is "X". The second player is "O". A player claims a square by marking the square with either "X" or "O", depending whose turn it is.

A player declares a square by entering a row number (with the top row as 0, middle row as 1, and bottom row as 2) followed by a column number (with the left column as 0, middle column as 1, and right column as 2).

If a player declares a square that is already declared, the game will display "invalid move" and the player should enter another choice.

The game is over when one player wins or when all squares have been declared.
Solution:

Step 1: Display the board.

Start a new project called Chapter5Example2. Add a new class called Board to the project. Type the code as shown in Figure 5.5.

The Board class has only one field called allCells, which is a two-dimensional array. This corresponds to the 3 by 3 game board.

The Board class has a ToString() method that will display the board with the content from allCells. A sample output looks like this:

```
E | X | E
E | O | E
E | E | E
```

```
1    namespace Chapter5Example2
2    {
         3 references
3        public enum CellValue { E, X, O }
         3 references
4        internal class Board
5        {
6            // field
7            private CellValue[,] allCells;
8            // property
             9 references
9            public CellValue[,] AllCells
10           {
11               get { return allCells; }
12               set { allCells = value; }
13           }
14           // constructor
             1 reference
15           public Board()
16           {
17               allCells = new CellValue[3, 3];
18           }
19           // ToString
             0 references
20           public override string ToString()
21           {
22               string str;
23               str = AllCells[0, 0] + " | " + AllCells[0, 1] + " | " + AllCells[0, 2]
24                   + "\n-----------\n" +
25                   AllCells[1, 0] + " | " + AllCells[1, 1] + " | " + AllCells[1, 2]
26                   + "\n-----------\n" +
27                   AllCells[2, 0] + " | " + AllCells[2, 1] + " | " + AllCells[2, 2];
28               return str;
29           }
30       }
31   }
```

Figure 5.5 Code for the Board class of Chapter5Example2.

Explanation:

Line 3 creates an enum type called CellValue, with possible values of E, X, and O.

Enumeration (enum) is a programmer defined type. It works like a constant variable, which you learned earlier can be more meaningful than a numeric literal. Enumeration prevents errors by not allowing programmers to type in anything other than what is defined. Declaring an enumeration is similar to declaring a class. Just replace the "class" keyword with the "enum" keyword. The content of an enum is much simpler. Just include all allowed values in a pair of curly braces.

Line 7 declares a two-dimensional array of CellValue type called allCells.

Line 17 creates a two-dimensional array of CellValue type. The size of the array is 3 by 3, meaning it has three rows and three columns. The rows count from 0 to 2. The same is true for columns. The memory address of this new array is assigned to the allCells array variable declared in Line 7. The default value of this array is E, because that's the first one on the CellValue enum type.

In Line 23 AllCells[0, 0] holds the value of row 0 (the first row) and column 0 (the first column). Similarly AllCells[0, 1] holds the value of row 0 (the first row) and column 1 (the second column).

In Line 24, \n is a new line symbol. It works like pressing the "Enter" key.

Next, in the default Main() method of the Program class, type in the code as shown in Figure 5.6.

```
1    namespace Chapter5Example2
2    {
         0 references
3        class Program
4        {
             0 references
5            static void Main()
6            {
7                Board board = new Board();
8                Console.WriteLine(board);
9            }
10       }
11   }
```

Figure 5.6 Code for the Main() method.

Save and run the program. You should see a console output as shown in Figure 5.7.

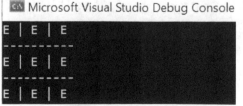

Figure 5.7 Output at the end of Step 1.

Step 2: Play forever.

We are going to change the letter E to X or O based on which player plays. After the first player (X) chooses the row and column numbers, that position will be replaced with X. Next, the second player (O) chooses a position to put O. The two players take turns to play forever. After all squares are declared, no valid play is possible.

Add a class called Player to the project. Replace the default code with the following:

```csharp
namespace Chapter5Example2
{
    internal class Player
    {
        // fields
        private CellValue playerName;
        private int row;
        private int column;
        // properties
        public CellValue PlayerName
        {
            get { return playerName; }
            set { playerName = value; }
        }
        public int Row
        {
            get { return row; }
            set { row = value; }
        }
        private int Column
        {
            get { return column; }
            set { column = value; }
        }
        // constructor
        public Player(CellValue playerName, int row, int column)
        {
            this.playerName = playerName;
            this.row = row;
            this.column = column;
        }
        // method
        public void PlayerMove(Board board)
        {
            board.AllCells[Row, Column] = PlayerName;
        }
    }
}
```

Explanation:
The PlayerMove() method updates the two dimensional array for the specific player.

Next, update the Main() method so it now looks like:

```
7                    Board board = new Board();
8                    Console.WriteLine(board);
9                    CellValue playerName = CellValue.X;
10                   int row;
11                   int col;
12                   bool playerWins = false;
13                   bool stalemate = false;
14                   while(!(playerWins || stalemate))
15                   {
16                       do
17                       {
18                           Console.WriteLine($"Player {playerName} moves.");
19                           Console.WriteLine("Enter row number (0, 1, 2):");
20                           row=int.Parse(Console.ReadLine()!);
21                           Console.WriteLine("Enter column number (0, 1, 2):");
22                           col=int.Parse(Console.ReadLine()!);
23                           if(board.AllCells[row, col] != CellValue.E)
24                               Console.WriteLine("Invalid move");
25                       } while (board.AllCells[row, col] != CellValue.E);
26                       Player player = new Player(playerName, row, col);
27                       player.PlayerMove(board);
28                       Console.WriteLine(board);
29                       playerName = (playerName == CellValue.X) ?
30                           CellValue.O : CellValue.X;
31                   }
```

Figure 5.8 The updated Main() method.

Explanation:

Line 9 initializes the first player (player X).

Lines 10 and 11 declare two variables to hold the row and column numbers entered by a player.

Lines 12 and 13 declare and initialize two variables to check if the game is over. The game is over when one player wins or all squares on the board are declared.

Lines 14 to 31 are a while loop that will run until the game is over. Because we don't know how to check if a player wins or if all squares on the board are declared, this loop will run forever.

Lines 16 to 25 is another loop nested inside the first loop that will run until the player enters a valid row and column number. A valid row and column number is a square that has the E value (empty). Line 26 instantiates a player object with the row and column chosen by the player.

Line 27 calls the PlayerMove() method to update the array value.

Line 28 displays the board with the new content.

Lines 29 and 30 change the player name. The ternary expression is the same as the following:

```
if (playerName == CellValue.X)
      playerName = CellValue.O;
else
      playerName = CellValue.X;
```

Save and run the program to see the X and Os replacing Es.

Step 3: Game over
You need to check if a player has won, or if all squares on the board have been declared (not E).

First, open the Player class in code view and add the IsPlayerWin() method below:

```
public bool IsPlayerWin(Board board)
{
  bool isWin = false;
  if(board.AllCells[0,0] !=CellValue.E &&
     board.AllCells[0,0] ==board.AllCells[1,1]&&
     board.AllCells[1, 1] == board.AllCells[2, 2])
  {
    isWin = true;
  }
  if(board.AllCells[0,2] !=CellValue.E &&
     board.AllCells[0,2] == board.AllCells[1,1] &&
     board.AllCells[1,1] == board.AllCells[2, 0])
  {
    isWin=true;
  }
  for(int r = 0; r < 3; r++)
  {
    if(board.AllCells[r, 0] != CellValue.E &&
       board.AllCells[r, 0] == board.AllCells[r, 1] &&
       board.AllCells[r, 1] == board.AllCells[r, 2])
    {
      isWin = true;
    }
  }
  for(int c= 0; c < 3; c++)
  {
      if(board.AllCells[0, c] != CellValue.E &&
```

```
        board.AllCells[0, c] == board.AllCells[1, c] &&
        board.AllCells[1, c] == board.AllCells[2, c])
    {
        isWin = true;
    }
   }
  return isWin;
 }
```

Explanation:

There are four situations in which a player wins: 1) the diagonal, from top left to bottom right are the same letter; 2) the diagonal, from top right to bottom left are the same letter; 3) any of the three rows are the same letter; 4) any of the three columns are the same letter. The IsPlayerWin() does exactly that.

Next, add the HasNoMoreE() method, as shown in Figure 5.9, inside the Board class. I suggest that you place the method right before the ToString() method.

```
                    1 reference
20                  public bool HasNoMoreE()
21                  {
22                      bool noMoreE = true;
23                      for (int r = 0; r < 3; r++)
24                      {
25                          for (int c = 0; c < 3; c++)
26                          {
27                              if (allCells[r, c] == CellValue.E)
28                                  noMoreE = false;
29                          }
30                      }
31                      return noMoreE;
32                  }
```

Figure 5.9 Code for HasNoMoreE() method.

Finally, add the code, as shown in Figure 5.10, inside the Main() method towards the end of the method right before the following line:

```
playerName = (playerName == CellValue.X)?
```

```
29        playerWins = player.IsPlayerWin(board);
30        stalemate = board.HasNoMoreE();
31        if (playerWins)
32            Console.WriteLine($"Player {playerName} wins.");
33        if (stalemate)
34            Console.WriteLine("Stalemate!");
```

Figure 5.10 Code for checking if a player won, or if all squares on the board have been declared.

Save and run the application to see how your Tic Tac Toe game works.

5.2 Agile Artifacts

As you learned in Chapter 2, there are three roles, five events, and three artifacts in scrum. You learned the agile roles and events in the previous two chapters. In this chapter, you will learn the three artifacts. The agile artifacts include product backlog, sprint backlog, and increments.

5.2.1 Product Backlog and User Story

The product backlog contains all software requirements in the form of user stories. The product backlog starts with rough software requirements. Over time, when more about the software is known and more increments are completed, the product backlog evolves.

Product Backlog
User Story 1 (most valuable and detailed)
User Story 2 (next valuable and detailed)
....
Epic (less detailed)
....
Theme (least detailed)

Figure 5.11 Product backlog with different priority and granularity levels.

User stories in the product backlog are organized with those of higher priority at the top and those of lower priority at the bottom (Figure 5.11). Priority is based on how much value the completed user story will add to the business. The product owner decides which user stories are the most valuable based on the value analysis.

Test Your Understanding 5.13
Which of the following statements about user stories are correct?
1) Product backlog contains user stories.
2) User stories are software requirements.
A. 1) only
B. 2) only
C. Both 1) and 2)
D. Neither 1) nor 2)

Test Your Understanding 5.14
User stories with higher priority should be _____ of the product backlog.
A. at the top
B. in the middle
C. at the bottom
D. anywhere

Test Your Understanding 5.15
User stories at the top of the product backlog are in _____ details.
A. normal
B. more
C. less
D. least

To determine business values, first determine the area the completed user story will affect (Marchewka, 2015). The following are areas affected:

1. Customer. These values are related to customers. For example, if the software functions or features can reduce product price, then the business value is in the customer area.

2. Strategic. If the completed user story can create new markets or increase the market share of the company, then the value is in the strategic area.

3. Financial. If the software can increase the return on investment or reduce the cost, then the value is in the financial area.

4. Operational. If the software can increase the efficiency and effectiveness of the company operation, the value is in the operational area.

5. Social. If the software can benefit society, such as dissemination of knowledge, or reduction of pollution, the value is in the social area.

Next, develop an appropriate metric to measure the business value. Not all values can be easily quantified, though business values in the financial area are relatively easy to quantify.

Test Your Understanding 5.16
Which of the following is NOT a business value area?
A. customer
B. financial
C. social
D. technical

Test Your Understanding 5.17
If the completed feature of the user story can create new markets for the company, the business value is in _____ area.
A. customer
B. financial
C. strategic
D. technical

Test Your Understanding 5.18
If the completed feature of the user story can reduce product price, the business value is in _____ area.
A. customer
B. social
C. strategic
D. technical

Another prioritization method is called MoSCow, outlined in the Dynamic Systems Development Method (DSDM) (Craddock et al., 2012), which is one of many agile approaches. MoSCow includes four priority levels:

1. Must haves: Requirements in this category must be implemented, otherwise the solution won't work or will be useless. These are the minimum components the team must deliver.

2. Should haves: Requirements in this category are important, but can be omitted if the schedule or budget won't permit.

3. Could haves: These requirements enhance the solution, but can be left out or are not critical.

4. Want to haves: These requirements are nice to have and can be included in later development. They are not included in the initial delivery.

Test Your Understanding 5.19
In MoSCow, which category includes requirements that are important, but can be omitted if the schedule or budget won't permit?
A. Must haves
B. Should haves
C. Could haves
D. Want to haves

Test Your Understanding 5.20
In MoSCow, which category includes requirements that are nice to have and can be included in the next development?
A. Must haves
B. Should haves
C. Could haves
D. Want to haves

Test Your Understanding 5.21
In MoSCow, which category includes the requirements that can enhance the solution, but can be left out or are not critical?
A. Must haves
B. Should haves
C. Could haves
D. Want to haves

Test Your Understanding 5.22
In MoSCow, which category includes requirements that must be implemented?
A. Must haves
B. Should haves
C. Could haves
D. Want to haves

As shown in Figure 5.16, not all user stories in the product backlog are in the same granularity (Patton, 2014). For those at the top of the list, greater detail is needed. Those at the bottom of the list may not even count as stories. They may instead be referred to as 'epics' or 'themes'. An epic is a user story that is too big to be designed, coded, or tested within a single sprint. A theme is a very general story or a big idea, sometimes containing the whole release or even multiple releases. Most requirements start out as themes or epics, since the first idea customers have for their software tend to be abstract. As the project progresses, stories will become more detailed to fit the work.

Test Your Understanding 5.23
User stories in the product backlog have different _____; stories with higher priority should have _____ details.
A. length, less
B. priority, less
C. details, less
D. granularity, more

Test Your Understanding 5.24
Items inside the product backlog have different granularity; the most general and abstract item is a _____.
A. general story
B. general item
C. abstract story
D. theme

Test Your Understanding 5.25
List items in the product backlog from least to most detailed.
A. user story, epic, theme
B. theme, epic, user story
C. epic, user story, theme
D. epic, theme. User story

You have seen the term "user story" many times, but what exactly is a user story? A user story includes a statement of the requirements and any acceptance criteria. A user story takes this format:

As a < type of user >, I want < some goal >, so that < some reason >

In our toy retailer example, a possible user story can be:

As a manager, I want to check the inventory level at any time so that I know when to place a replenishment.

A user story is written on an index card, implying it shouldn't be too long or complicated.

Acceptance criteria is written on the back of the user story (Cohn, 2004). The criteria include assumptions made by the customers. In the retailer example, the manager may state that he wants to be able to check the inventory by product id, product name, and partial product name, and be able to view all products on one screen.

The criteria can also be used to determine if a story is fully implemented. From the same example, the manager may simply want all inventory information to be displayed on one screen and be able to print it off onto paper.

Test Your Understanding 5.26

Which of the following is NOT a component of a user story?
A. user
B. goal
C. platform
D. reason

Test Your Understanding 5.27
A user story should be written on an index card so that it is _____.
A. short and handy
B. short and simple
C. cost less and handy
D. cost less and simple

To write a good user story, you must follow the INVEST acronym (Cohn, 2010):

Independent: The user story must be able to stand alone. Ideally, user stories can be delivered in any order.
Negotiable: A user story is a conversation, not a specification. Collaboration and discussion about the best way to solve the business problem should happen between the product owner and the development team.
Valuable: A user story should provide business values to the company, as you learned earlier in this

chapter.

Estimable: A user story must be detailed enough that a team can estimate the amount of effort needed to complete it.

Small: A story should be small enough to fit into a single sprint.

Testable: If a story is not testable, it is too vague.

Test Your Understanding 5.28
A user story is a conversation, not a specification. This is _____ in the INVEST acronym.
A. independent
B. negotiable
C. valuable
D. estimable

Test Your Understanding 5.29
A user story should not be vague. This is _____ in the INVEST acronym.
A. independent
B. negotiable
C. small
D. testable

User stories in the product backlog must be estimated. If not all stories are estimated, at least those stories at the top should be estimated. Estimation is about predicting how much effort will be required to complete the story by the development team. It is measured by story points and determined by the development team. Many development teams estimate effort by using the planning poker game (Rubin, 2013):

Each team member has a stack of cards with the numbers ½, 1, 2, 3, 5, 8, 13, 20, 40, and 100. A story is then picked. The team reads the story and discusses it. Then, independently, team members place a card face down indicating how much effort they think the story will be. Values correspond to difficulty level. All cards are flipped over at the same time. The members with the smallest and largest values should explain their reasoning. The game is repeated until all numbers are relatively similar. Then, the team can select a number for the story.

Story points reflect the team's estimate for how much effort is needed to complete the story. It is a relative number. In other words, the story points for one team cannot be compared to the story points of another team.

Test Your Understanding 5.30
Which of the following statements about story points is correct?
1) When estimating a user story with the planning poker game, the average of all members' card face values is used as the story's points.
2) If Team A estimates 40 points, and Team B estimates 20 points for the same user story, one can conclude that Team B can complete the story in about half the time of Team A.
A. 1) only
B. 2) only
C. Both 1) and 2)
D. Neither 1) nor 2)

Before closing our discussion about the product backlog, let us consider the characteristics of a good product backlog, according to the DEEP principle (Cohn, 2010).

Detailed appropriately: Higher priority stories contain more details than lower priority stories.

Estimated: User stories in the product backlog should be estimable by the development team. This indicates the team can understand the stories. At the very least, stories at the top should be estimable.

Emergent: Stories in the product backlog are constantly evolving. When more about the marketplace is known, or technology advancement takes place, the product backlog should be updated. The product backlog is also updated between the sprints.

Prioritized: All stories should be prioritized based on the business value a story provides.

Test Your Understanding 5.31
Which of the following is NOT a characteristic of a good product backlog?
A. Detailed appropriately
B. Length appropriately
C. Estimate
D. Prioritized

Test Your Understanding 5.32
Stories in the product backlog are constantly evolving. This is a property of _____.
A. detailed appropriately

B. estimate
C. emergent
D. prioritized

5.2.2 Sprint Backlog

The sprint backlog contains items from the product backlog selected by the development team for the current sprint. It also includes any items added in the sprint planning meeting, such as the sprint goal. It is a forecast by the development team about what features will be included in the next increment, and the work needed to complete the features. The stories from the product backlog are often picked based on the team velocity (the number of story points the team can complete in one sprint).

The stories in the sprint backlog are broken down into sprint tasks, which are small enough to be assigned to one member as a day's work or less. Every sprint task is then estimated for the number of hours needed to complete it. User stories in the product backlog are estimated for effort in story points, while tasks in the sprint backlog are estimated by hours. As a result, each story in the sprint backlog also has a time estimate. Note that the relationship between story points and time estimates are not linear. In other words, if a 20 points story takes 200 hours, it does not mean that a 40 points story will take 400 hours. Story points are relative numbers while task estimates are absolute. Table 5.1 shows a comparison between product backlog and sprint backlog

Items	Product Backlog	Sprint Backlog
Scope	Project	Sprint
Detail	Less	More
Measurement	Story point	Hour
Ownership	Product owner	Team
Update Frequency	Weekly	Daily

Table 5.1 Comparison between Product Backlog and Sprint Backlog

Test Your Understanding 5.33
Stories in the product backlog are estimated by _____ while the tasks in the sprint backlog are
estimated by _____.
A. cost, hours
B. cost, effort
C. story points, hours
D. story points, effort

5.2.3 Increment

The increment is the piece of software containing all currently completed and tested items. All
increments must be completed to be 'done' and accepted by the product owner. Thus, the increment
gets larger and larger as more sprints are completed. The increment of the last sprint of the project is
the whole, completed software the customer asked for.

Test Your Understanding 5.34
An increment is all the items completed in one sprint.
A. TRUE
B. FALSE

Test Your Understanding 5.35
The increment of the last sprint is _____.
A. a milestone
B. a closure
C. the final sprint
D. the software the customer wants

5.3 Chapter Summary

In this chapter, you learned that a C# class is a logical group of methods and the data that these
methods work on. When you think of a class, you think of its status and behavior. The status is the
fields, and the behavior is the methods. Most classes will include fields, properties, constructors,
normal methods, and ToString() methods.

You also learned the three artifacts of scrum: product backlog, sprint backlog, and increment. The
product backlog contains all user stories, epics, and themes. The sprint backlog are stories picked from
the product backlog by the team to be in the current sprint backlog, plus additional items agreed upon

by the team during sprint planning. The increment is the accumulated parts of software after each sprint.

5.4 References

Cohn, M. (2004). User Stories Applied for Agile Software Development, Addison-Wesley. Boston.

Cohn, M. (2006). Agile estimating and planning. Prentice Hall. Upper Saddle River, NJ.

Cohn, M. (2010). Succeeding with Agile: Software development using Scrum. Addison-Wesley. Boston, MA.

Craddock, A., Roberts, B., Richards, K. Godwin, J., and Tudor, D. (2012), The DSDM Agile Project Framework for Scrum. DSDM consortium.

Marchewka, J. T. (2015), *Information Technology Project Management*, 5th Edition. Wiley.

Patton, J. (2014), User Story Mapping Discover the whole story, Build the Right Product. O'Reilly. Sebastopol, CA.

Rubin, K.S. (2013). Essential Scrum A Practical Guide to the Most Popular Agile Process, Addison-Wesley. Boston.

5.5 Solutions to Test Your Understanding

5.1 A; 5.2 D; 5.3 B; 5.4 B; 5.5 A; 5.6 A; 5.7 C; 5.8 A; 5.9 D; 5.10 B; 5.11 A; 5.12 C; 5.13 C; 5.14 A; 5.15 B; 5.16D; 5.17 C; 5.18 A; 5.19 B; 5.20 D; 5.21 C; 5.22 A; 5.23 D; 5.24 D; 5.25 B; 5.26 C; 5.27 B; 5.28 B; 5.29 D; 5.30 D; 5.31 B; 5.32 C; 5.33 C; 5.34 B.5.35 D.

Chapter 6: C# Inheritance and Agile Metrics

6.1 Inheritance

In the last chapter, you learned how to create your own custom classes and how to instantiate a class to use its methods. What if the two classes you need to create are very similar? You can create two classes anyway. However, since there are many duplicated fields and methods, there is a better way to do it. Put all those common fields and methods from those two classes in a third class called 'super type' and let the two classes, known as sub type, inherit all elements from the super type.

Instead of creating two classes, you end up with writing three classes. Since all common members are now in the super class, the two sub classes are now simpler. This also enhances the maintenance. If you need to update one common member while using the two classes approach, you would have to update in two places. If you use the three classes approach, you only have to update in one location.

Example 6.1

Problem:

At Tiny College, both undergraduate and graduate students have a student ID, a student name, and a numeric grade score between 0 and 100. However, undergraduates have letter grades (A, B, C, D, and

F) with pluses and minuses, while graduates only have a letter. Create three classes: one super class called Student and two sub classes called Undergraduate and Graduate respectively.

Demonstrate the classes you created with four students, two undergraduates and two graduates in the Main() method.

```
Microsoft Visual Studio Debug Console
Name: Lynn Score: 98 Letter grade: A
Name: Bob Score: 88 Letter grade: B+
Name: Chuck Score: 76 Letter grade: C
Name: Dan Score: 56 Letter grade: F
```

Analysis:

In this example, you don't see many problems with the two-class approach. However, when there are many fields and methods, you would see a lot of duplications. Duplication not only creates extra typing for the programmers, it also causes nightmares when maintaining the code. For example, when Tiny College wants to keep more student records, it decides to separate a student's name into first and last. To achieve this, you would have to recode in all related classes. It is almost guaranteed that something will be omitted. Companies often wind up paying consulting firms to fix these costly, accumulated problems.

A better approach is to create a super class called Student that contains all common elements of both the undergraduate class and graduate class and to let both sub classes inherit from the super class. A Unified Modeling Language (UML) class diagram is displayed in Figure 6.1.

A class diagram uses a rectangle box to represent a class, with all fields, properties, and methods inside the box. It uses the empty arrow head to show the inheritance relationship. The arrow points to the super class from the sub class. The inheritance relationship is often called an "is-a" relationship, because a sub type "is-a" super type.

The super class is often called base class and the sub class is often called derived class.

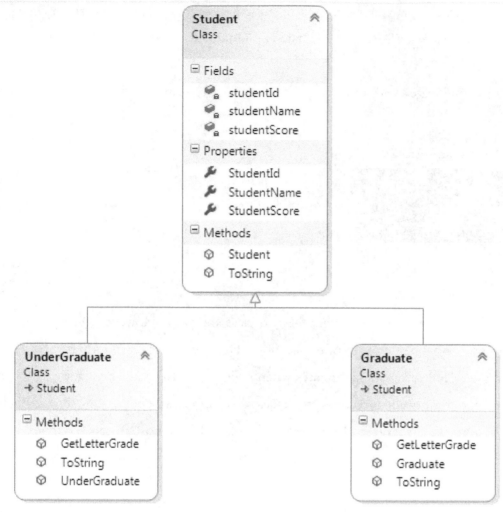

Figure 6.1 UML class diagram

As you can see from the diagram, neither Undergraduate nor Graduate classes need to repeat the common fields and properties. They just need those unique member elements. When a change is needed for student name, only the Student class needs to be updated. This avoids many potential errors.

Test Your Understanding 6.1
Which of the following statements about inheritance is correct?
1) A super class contains all the common fields and methods of the sub classes so that the sub classes don't need to include those members.
2) A super class is often called derived class and a sub class is often called base class.

A. 1) only
B. 2) only
C. Both 1) and 2)
D. Neither1) nor 2)

Test Your Understanding 6.2
The relationship between the super type and sub type in an inheritance is often called an _____
relationship.
A. super-sub
B. belongs to
C. has-a
D. is-a

Test Your Understanding 6.3
A diagram with rectangles to represent classes with fields, properties, and methods inside the box and
arrows showing the relationships is a(n) _____ class diagram.
A. UML
B. CML
C. UCL
D. UMC

Solution:

Step 1. Add the Student class:

Create a console app called Chapter6Example1. Right click on the project in the "Solution Explorer"

window, and add a new class called "Student". In the Student Class, nothing new is introduced. Just

type the code as shown below:


```
namespace Chapter6Example1
{
    internal class Student
    {
        // fields
        private string studentId;
        private string name;
        private int score;
        // properties
        public string StudentId
        {
            get { return studentId; }
```

```csharp
            set { studentId = value; }
        }
        public string Name
        {
            get { return name; }
            set { name = value; }
        }
        public int Score
        {
            get { return score; }
            set { score = value; }
        }
        // constructor
        public Student(string studentId, string name, int score)
        {
            this.studentId = studentId;
            this.name = name;
            this.score = score;
        }
        public override string ToString()
        {
            string str;
            str = $"Name: {Name} Score: {Score}";
            return str;
        }
    }
}
```

Step 2. Add the Undergraduate class:

Next, right click on the project Chapter6Example1 in the "Solution Explorer" window again to add a new class called "Undergraduate.cs". Add the code as shown below:

```csharp
namespace Chapter6Example1
{
    internal class Undergraduate: Student
    {
        // constructor
        public Undergraduate(string studentId, string name, int score)
            : base(studentId, name, score)
        {
        }
        // method
        public string GetLetterGrade()
```

```
    {
        string letterGrade;
        if (Score >= 94)
            letterGrade = "A";
        else if (Score >= 90)
            letterGrade = "A-";
        else if (Score >= 87)
            letterGrade = "B+";
        else if (Score >= 84)
            letterGrade = "B";
        else if (Score >= 80)
            letterGrade = "B-";
        else if (Score >= 77)
            letterGrade = "C+";
        else if (Score >= 74)
            letterGrade = "C";
        else if (Score >= 70)
            letterGrade = "C-";
        else if (Score >= 67)
            letterGrade = "D+";
        else if (Score >= 64)
            letterGrade = "D";
        else if (Score >= 60)
            letterGrade = "D-";
        else
            letterGrade = "F";
        return letterGrade;
    }
    //ToString
    public override string ToString()
    {
        string str;
        str = base.ToString() + $" Letter grade: {GetLetterGrade()}";
        return str;
    }
    }
}
```

To make Undergraduate class a derived class of the Student class, add :Student to the Undergraduate class header, like this:

```
internal class Undergraduate: Student
```

Additionally, the Undergraduate class constructor can call the base class constructor by :base. The constructor of the Undergraduate class is:

```
public Undergraduate(string studentId, string name, int score)
    : base(studentId, name, score)
```

```
{
}
```

This indicates the three arguments are passed to the base class constructor. In other words, the current constructor will not do anything to those three parameters. The base class constructor will handle it. It calls the base class constructor by passing arguments for the fields in the base class. If any fields that are in the derived class and not in the base class, the derived class should still handle them.

Inside the ToString method, the base.ToString() will call the ToString() method in the base class and adds content there.

Test Your Understanding 6.4
Which of the following statements about class inheritance is correct?
1) If Class A inherits from Class B, you don't need to do anything on Class B.
2) If Class A inherits from Class B, you should add :B in the Class A header to indicate Class A inherits from Class B.
A. 1) only
B. 2) only
C. Both 1) and 2)
D. Neither 1) nor 2)

Test Your Understanding 6.5
Constructors in a sub class often need to call the super class constructor by using :_____.
A. base()
B. super()
C. sub()
D. derived()

Step 3. Add the Graduate class:

Next, right click on the project Chapter6Example1 in the "Solution Explorer" window again to add a new class called "Graduate.cs". Add the code as shown below:

```
namespace Chapter6Example1
{
    internal class Graduate:Student
    {
        // constructor
        public Graduate(string studentId, string name, int score)
```

```
        :base(studentId, name, score)
    {


    }
    // method
    public string GetLetterGrade()
    {
        string letterGrade;
        if (Score >= 90)
            letterGrade = "A";
        else if(Score >=80)
            letterGrade = "B";
        else if(Score >= 70)
            letterGrade= "C";
        else if(Score >=60)
            letterGrade= "D";
        else
            letterGrade= "F";
        return letterGrade;
    }
    public override string ToString()
    {
        string str;
        str = base.ToString() + $" Letter grade: {GetLetterGrade()}";
        return str;
    }
  }
}
```

Step 4. Demonstrate the classes in the Main() method.

Finally, in the "Solution Explorer" window, open the "Program.cs" in code view, replace the default code with the following:

```
namespace Chapter6Example1
{
  public class Program
  {
    static void Main()
    {
        List<Student> students = new List<Student>();
        Undergraduate ud1 = new Undergraduate("111", "Lynn", 98);
        students.Add(ud1);
        Undergraduate ud2 = new Undergraduate("222", "Bob", 88);
        students.Add(ud2);
        Graduate g1 = new Graduate("333", "Chuck", 76);
        students.Add(g1);
```

```
        Graduate g2 = new Graduate("444", "Dan", 56);
        students.Add(g2);
        foreach(Student student in students)
        {
            Console.WriteLine(student);
        }
    }
  }
}
```

Explanation:

The following line creates a list:

List<Student> students = new List<Student>();

A List is almost the same as an array, but a List is more convenient to use. A List has more methods and can expand as needed. This line declares a List called students that can hold any number of Students. The class name in the bracket <Student> indicates the List will hold only the Student type. Because both undergraduate and graduate inherits from Student, we say the relationship is an "is a" relationship. In other words, an undergraduate is a student, and a graduate is a student too. As a result, both Undergraduate and Graduate can be stored in the students list.

Using Student to represent both undergraduate and graduate is called polymorphism in object-oriented programming. Polymorphism means "multiple forms". In this example, Student can have "two forms", an undergraduate or a graduate.

The following line:

students.Add(ud1);

Add an undergraduate object to the list by using the pre-built method "Add" of the List class.

Test Your Understanding 6.6
The statement, List<Student> students = new List<Student>(); will create a list called students that can only hold references to _____.
A. a student type, not any other types
B. an undergraduate type only
C. a graduate type only
D. a student type and its derived types

Test Your Understanding 6.7

If the Graduate class inherits from the Student class, then, anywhere in the code, when a Student object is expected, a Graduate object can be used. This is called _____.
A. encapsulation
B. polymorphism
C. inheritance
D. representation

Test Your Understanding 6.8
A List in C# is similar to an array that can be used to hold a group of values. However, a List is more convenient because _____.
A. it has more methods, and it runs faster
B. it can expand as needed, and it runs faster
C. it has more methods, and it can expand as needed
D. it is more concise

Test Your Understanding 6.9
To add an element to a List, you can use the _____ method of the List class.
A. Add()
B. Include()
C. Element()
D. AddElement()

Programming Challenge 6.1

The Tiny Company has two types of employees: fulltime and parttime. Both types have an employee ID and employee name. Fulltime employees have a salary, and parttime employees have an hourly wage and hours worked.

A full time employee gets paid weekly by dividing the salary by 52 while a part time employee gets paid by the product of hourly wage and hours worked.

Specifically, you will create an Employee class with the common elements (employee ID, employee name, ToString() method). Then create a Fulltime employee class with a salary field and the GetWeeklyPaid() method. Similarly, create a Parttime employee class with hourly wage and hours worked fields and the GetWeeklyPaid() method. Add appropriate properties, constructors, and ToString() methods. Each class should be in its own cs file.

Finally, demonstrate the classes in the Main() method of the Program class with data made up for two full time employees and two part time employees in a List of Employee. Display the employee's payment data in a foreach loop.

6.2 Abstract Method and Abstract Class

In Example 6.1, you may notice that both Graduate and Undergraduate sub classes have a GetLetterGrade() method that is not in the super class. Why is a common method not in the super class? This is because they have different implementations. However, a better design is to put the GetLetterGrade() method in the super class as an abstract method.

We have to make the GetLetterGrade() method in the super class as abstract because we don't have any implementations for that method. The implementation depends on whether a student is a graduate or undergraduate. An abstract method has only a method header without a method body, not even the pair of curly braces. The abstract method terminated with a semicolon.

Example 6.2

Problem:

Continue to work on Example 6.1 by adding an abstract method called GetLetterGrade to the Student class. Make necessary modification to the code so that the app work as Example 6.1

Solution:

Make a copy of Chapter6Example1 project folder. Rename the folder to Chapter6Example2. Do not rename anything inside the folder. Open the app in the new folder in Visual Studio. Inside the Student class, add the following abstract method right before the ToString() method:

```
public abstract string GetLetterGrade();
```

You will notice that the method name has a red squiggly line. If you point your mouse over it, you will see why.

```
GetLetterGrade();
```

```
     string Student.GetLetterGrade()

'Student.GetLetterGrade()' is abstract but it is contained in non-abstract class 'Student'
```

The error message tells you that you must make the class abstract because you now have an abstract method. Therefore, add the keyword "abstract" right before the "class Student" in the class header, like this:

```
internal abstract class Student
```

Note that an abstract class cannot be instantiated, or cannot have objects. In other words, Tiny College can have graduate or undergraduate students, but cannot have any categorized as simply 'students'.

The Student class is now free of errors. However, both the UnderGraduate and Graduate classes have errors. This is because when a sub class inherits from an abstract super class, all abstract methods in the super class must be overridden or kept abstract. Go to both derived classes and add the "override" keyword to the GetLetterGrade() methods:

```
public override string GetLetterGrade()
```

Save and run the program. You should see the same output as Example 6.1 on the console screen.

The benefit of adding an abstract method in the super class without implementation is that you can be sure that all sub classes have that method with its own implementation. In our example, you can be sure that all sub classes from the Student class have a GetLetterGrade() method. No programmers can "forget" to add that method in a sub class.

In class inheritance, you must override an abstract method in the base class. Can you override an ordinary method in the base class in order to have a different implementation? No. If you have such a need, you can set the method in the base class as virtual. Suppose you have a method in the base class:

```
public virtual string Greeting()
{
  return "Good morning.";
}
```

You can override it in the derived class like this:

```
public override string Greeting()
{
  return "Good afternoon.";
}
```

The keyword "override" in the Greeting method allows the Greeting method to behave differently than its parent's method with the same name, same parameters (this is called method signature), and same return type.

In summary, an abstract method in the base class must be overridden in the derived class or kept abstract. A virtual method in the base class can be overridden in the derived class. A normal method in the base class cannot be overridden in the derived class.

Test Your Understanding 6.10
Which of the following statements about override is correct?
1) In C#, a virtual method in the super class can be overridden by a method in the sub class if a different implementation is used in the sub class.
2) in C#, an abstract method in the super class can be overridden by a method in the sub class if a different implementation is used in the sub class.
A. 1) only
B. 2) only
C. Both 1) and 2)
D. Neither 1) nor 2)

Test Your Understanding 6.11
Which of the following statements about override is correct?
1) In C#, a virtual method in the super class must be overridden by a method in the sub class.
2) In C#, any method in the super class can be overridden by a sub class if a different implementation is used in the sub class.
A. 1) only
B. 2) only
C. Both 1) and 2)
D. Neither 1) nor 2)

Test Your Understanding 6.12
When a method in the sub class overrides a method in the super class, the two methods must have the same _____.
A. access modifier
B. return type
C. parameter list
D. signature

Test Your Understanding 6.13
A method's name and parameter lists are often called a method's _____.
A. header
B. Main
C. signature
D. method body

Test Your Understanding 6.14
If a class in C# has an abstract method, the class must _____.
A. have a corresponding overloaded method
B. have a corresponding overridden method

C. have no other method(s)

D. be abstract

Test Your Understanding 6.15

A benefit of adding an abstract method in the super class without implementation is _____.

A. for the backward compatibility

B. flexibility

C. that you can be sure that all sub classes have that method with its own implementation.

D. code brevity

Test Your Understanding 6.16

Unlike a concrete class, an abstract class cannot _____.

A. be instantiated

B. be updated

C. have fields

D. have non abstract methods

Test Your Understanding 6.17

When a sub class inherits from an abstract super class, all abstract methods in the super class must be _____.

A. overridden

B. overloaded

C. overridden or kept abstract.

D. overloaded or kept abstract

Programming Challenge 6.2

Make a copy of the Program Challenge 6.1 project folder. Open the app of the new folder in Visual Studio. With Employee class in code view, add GetWeeklyPaid() abstract method to the class. Make all necessary changes so that the program can still run as expected.

6.3 Interface

Interface is similar to an abstract class, but it plays a very different role. A superclass defines common behavior for related subclasses. For example, a super class called Student can be used for all types of student to inherit, but not for faculty. An interface, on the other hand, can be used to define common behaviors for any classes (including unrelated classes; for example, both students and faculty can set up an email account). Additionally, a class can only inherit from one other class, but can implement many interfaces.

An interface is like a contract that if a class implements this interface, it meets all the requirements of the interface. In everyday life, suppose you want to buy a plug for an outlet of a new house. You would need to find out about the pins, voltages, etc. Or, if you know the type follows the US Department of Commerce International Trade Administration (ITA) standard, you can buy the same type of plug and be sure they will match. You can think of the type by ITA as an interface. Even though ITA does not make any outlets or plugs, if a plug and an outlet meet the ITA's type standard, you can be sure they will match.

Interfaces define a specific set of functionalities without having to provide any details. Any class that implements the interface has to provide the details and make the methods work. Different classes implementing the same interface can have different implementations of the same functionality. For example, both credit cards and debit cards have a "make a purchase" functionality, but credit card purchases increase balance while debit card purchases decrease balance.

Example 6.3

Problem:

Continue Example 6.1 for Tiny College. Create an interface called IRegistration with two properties: parttimeMaxHours and fulltimeMaxHours , and two methods: checkPrerequisite() and addClass(). Next, create a class called ParttimeStudent that inherits from Graduate and implements IRegistration interface.
Finally, demonstrate the ParttimeStudent in the Main() method.

Solution:
Copy Chapter6Example1 project folder and rename it to Chapter6Example3. Open the app of the new folder in Visual Studio. In the "Solution Explorer" window, right click on the "Chapter6Example1" project. Select "Add", then select "New Item". In the middle panel of the popup "Add new item" window, select "Interface", then type in "IRegistration.cs" in the "Name" field at the bottom. Refer to Figure 6.2 for details.

Figure 6.2 Add New Item window

Click on the "Add" button to have a blank interface.

Use the code below for the IRegistration interface.

```
namespace Chapter6Example1
{
    internal interface IRegistration
    {
        int ParttimeMaxHours { get; set; }
        int FulltimeMaxHours { get; set;}
        bool CheckPrerequisite();
        string AddClass();
    }
}
```

Explanation:

You may notice that there is no access modifier for any property or method in an interface. Also, a method does not have a body as an abstract method does. All members of an interface are public and abstract by default. Additionally, interfaces cannot have data fields. By convention, all interface names begin with the capital letter "I".

Next, add a class called ParttimeStudent to the project. Use the code below:

```csharp
namespace Chapter6Example1
{
    internal class ParttimeStudent:Graduate, IRegistration
    {
        // constructor
        public ParttimeStudent(string studentId, string name, int score)
            :base(studentId, name, score)
        {
        }
        public int ParttimeMaxHours { get; set; } = 6;
        public int FulltimeMaxHours { get; set; } = 18;
        public string AddClass()
        {
            if (CheckPrerequisite())
                return "Class added.";
            else
                return "Prerequisite not met.";
        }
        public bool CheckPrerequisite()
        {
            if(GetLetterGrade() == "A")
                return true;
            return false;
        }
    }
}
```

Explanation:

The following line:
    internal class ParttimeStudent:Graduate, IRegistration
indicates that the ParttimeStudent class inherits from the Graduate class and implements the

IRegistration interface.

The following line:

        public int ParttimeMaxHours { get; set; } = 6;
sets the default value for ParttimeMaxHours property at 6.

Finally, update the Main() method of the Program class by adding (updating) two part time students

and display if they can add a class. The updated Main method content looks like:

```csharp
List<Student> students = new List<Student>();
Undergraduate ud1 = new Undergraduate("111", "Lynn", 98);
students.Add(ud1);
Undergraduate ud2 = new Undergraduate("222", "Bob", 88);
```

```
students.Add(ud2);
Graduate g1 = new Graduate("333", "Chuck", 76);
students.Add(g1);
Graduate g2 = new Graduate("444", "Dan", 56);
students.Add(g2);
ParttimeStudent p1 = new ParttimeStudent("555", "Franklin", 88);
ParttimeStudent p2 = new ParttimeStudent("666", "Gray", 99);
students.Add(p1);
students.Add(p2);
foreach (Student student in students)
{
    Console.WriteLine(student);
    if (student is ParttimeStudent)
        Console.WriteLine(((ParttimeStudent)student).AddClass());
}
```

Explanation:

The following lines:
```
    if (student is ParttimeStudent)
        Console.WriteLine(((ParttimeStudent)student).AddClass());
```
Check if the student object is a ParttimeStudent type. If yes, then include the AddClass() method.

(ParttimeStudent)s down casts the objects to ParttimeStudent from a Student type so that you can use the AddClass() method.

Save and run the program. A sample output looks like:

```
Microsoft Visual Studio Debug Console
Name: Lynn Score: 98 Letter grade: A
Name: Bob Score: 88 Letter grade: B+
Name: Chuck Score: 76 Letter grade: C
Name: Dan Score: 56 Letter grade: F
Name: Franklin Score: 88 Letter grade: B
Prerequisite not met.
Name: Gray Score: 99 Letter grade: A
Class added.
```

Test Your Understanding 6.18
An interface is like a _____ . If a class implements this interface, it meets all the requirements of the interface.
A. method
B. contract
C. window
D. field

Test Your Understanding 6.19
All members of an interface are _____ by default.
A. public and abstract
B. private and abstract
C. public and static
D. private and static

Test Your Understanding 6.20
In C#, an interface cannot have _____.
A. data fields
B. properties
C. methods
D. both properties and methods in the same interface

Test Your Understanding 6.21
Which of the following statements about interface naming is correct?
A. all interface names must begin with a lowercase "i"
B. all interface names must begin with the uppercase "I"
C. by convention, all interface names begin with a lowercase "i"
D. by convention, all interface names begin with the uppercase "I"

Programming Challenge 6.3
Copy Programming Challenge 6.1 project folder and rename it to Programming Challenge 6.3. Open the app of the new folder in Visual Studio. Add an interface called IMinimumWage with a property for state minimum hourly wage and a method called MetMinimum that returns true if the wage meets the minimum.
Next, add a class called CommissionEmployee that inherits from ParttimeEmployee and implements an IMinimumWage interface. A commission employee has a name, weekly sales amount, commission rate, and weekly hours worked. A commission employee is paid by weekly sales amount multiplied by the commission rate.

Finally, update the Main method to demonstrate the CommissionEmployee class by creating two commission employees: one that meets the minimum wage and one that does not.

6.4 Agile Metrics

Metrics are good communication tools that allow both stakeholders and team members to know where they are and how well they are doing (Broadus, 2013). Such communication is a success factor for agile project management (Tilk, 2016). In this section, we introduce three metrics. They are the Kanban board, burn down chart, and information radiator.

6.4.1 Kanban Board

You learned the concept of Kanban in Chapter Two. Every user story is written on one card, and each card is posted under one category to indicate the current status of that user story. A card will be rearranged after the status changes. This Kanban provides a visual representation of the software development status.

Agile teams often use a white board or simply the wall with sticky notes. The board is separated into five regions as shown in Figure 6.3:

Figure 6.3 A Sample Kanban Board

Backlog category: The product owner is in charge of this category. A user story is written on a sticky note and posted in the order of priority. Each story also contains a story point estimated by the development team. Depending on the size of the project, the list can be long and the product owner may update the category as needed, usually between the sprints.

Ready category: Stories in this category are in the hands of the development team. The stories are picked from the backlog category and are for the current sprint. Because each story usually should be broken down into multiple tasks, a sticky note from this column and any notes to the right of the same row will represent the different tasks of the same story. Estimation of the story is also changed from story points to time units, such as hours. There can be multiple tasks (sticky notes) on each row to represent the tasks for that story.

Development category: The development team is working on these tasks.

Test category: The development team is testing on these tasks to make sure the code is working as expected.

Done category: The tasks in this column are considered ready to be delivered to a customer. When all tasks of a user story are in this column, the sticky note that represents the user story is moved to this column.

Each column identifies a key hand-off or milestone for the tasks as a story is moved from one column to the next. Holding daily scrum meetings in front of the Kanban board makes the meeting more effective and also facilitates information sharing among the team members (Dinsmore and Cabanis-Brewin, 2014). Each member can easily see what the rest of the team are working on.

The Kanban board allows for quick feedback on potential issues. For example, if two members are working on the same column of the same row, they can discuss with each other to avoid interrupting each other's work. Also, the member working on the next column can estimate what task will come next and thus plan ahead.

In addition to providing a visual presentation of the project workflow, the major idea is to limit the number of stories that are a work-in-process (WIP), especially in the development and test columns (Ordysinski, 2013) so that bottlenecks can be identified. If more than a minimum number of WIPs are in a column, other members should take the opportunity to step up and assist.

Test Your Understanding 6.22

A sticky note on the ready category of a Kanban board usually represents a _____.

A. category

B. brief note
C. task
D. user story

Test Your Understanding 6.23
Which of the following is NOT an agile metric?
A. Kanban board
B. Burn-down chart
C. information radiator
D. user stories

Test Your Understanding 6.24
Metrics are good _____ that allow both stakeholders and team members to know where they are and how well they are doing.
A. status checks
B. measurements
C. reporting tools
D. communication tools

Test Your Understanding 6.25
Which of the following statements about user story is correct?
1) Except for the Backlog column, each row in a Kanban board represents a user story.
2) A user story is often estimated in hours, and a task of a user story is often estimated by story points.
A. 1) only
B. 2) only
C. Both 1) and 2)
D. Neither 1) nor 2)

Test Your Understanding 6.26
Which of the following is NOT a benefit of using Kanban?
A. visual representation of the status
B. identifying any bottlenecks
C. code transparency
D. communication metrics

6.4.2 Burn-Down Charts

A burn-down chart has two axes. The horizontal axis displays the number of days in the sprint, with larger numbers on the left and smaller numbers on the right. The vertical axis displays the number of hours left. Some teams display the number of hours left for the whole project, while some teams just display it for one sprint. This book follows the latter.

Let us explain how to draw a burn-down chart with an example. Suppose a team has 3 members, and each member works 8 hours a day, 5 days a week, and a sprint is time-boxed at 2 weeks. The team has 10 days marked on the horizontal axis and 240 hours (3x8x5x2 = 240) on the vertical axis. When there are 10 days left, there are 240 hours' worth of tasks left. When there are 9 days left, there are 216 hours' worth of tasks left. When there are 8 days left, there are 192 hours' worth of tasks left. Continuing with this trend, when there is 1 day left, there are 24 hours' worth of tasks left. When there are zero days left, there are zero hours' worth of tasks left. This is called a perfect burn down line or a planned burn down line. This line represents the ideal situation and is used for comparison purposes. Figure 6.4 displays the planned burn down chart.

Figure 6.4 Planned Burn Down Chart

On the same chart, let's draw another line to reflect the team's actual burn down. Suppose after the first day of work, the team completes 30 hours' worth of tasks. Mark the chart with (9, 210). Then there are two points on the chart. In the beginning of the sprint, there are always 240 hours' worth of tasks left (10, 240), and on 9 days left, there are 210 hours' worth of tasks left. Figure 6.5 shows the result after one day's work.

Figure 6.5 The burn down chart after one day's work.

Continue to draw the burn down chart for the team. Suppose on the second day (8 days left), the team completes another 35 hours' worth of tasks. Now there are only 175 (210-35) hours left. The new point is (8, 175). Figure 6.6 displays the burn down chart after two days' work.

Figure 6.6 The burn down chart after two days' work.

Suppose, on the third day (7 days left), the team completes only 20 hours' worth of tasks. Now there are only 155 (175-20) hours left. The new point is (7, 155). Figure 6.7 displays the burn down chart after three days' work by the team.

Figure 6.7 The burn down chart after three days' work.

You should have no difficulty completing the chart as the team completes more work until the end of the sprint.

A word of warning: it is possible for the actual line to go up when something went wrong (Vanderjack, 2015). For example, a task might've been underestimated. In general, if the "actual" line is under the "planned" line, the team is ahead of schedule, as shown in the figures. However, if the "actual" line is above the "planned" line for several days, the team must determine if they are able to finish the planned amount of work within the sprint.

Test Your Understanding 6.27

Which of the following statements about burn down charts is correct?

1) In a burn down chart, the horizontal axis represents the number of hours left, and the vertical axis represents the number of days left in the sprint.

2) The perfect burn down line is a straight line from top left to bottom right.

A. 1) only

B. 2) only

C. Both 1) and 2)

D. Neither 1) nor 2)

Test Your Understanding 6.28

Which of the following statements about burn down charts is correct?

1) To draw the burn down chart, at the end of each day, the team finds a point that represents how many days are left and how many hours' worth of work are left and connect that point to the existing trend.

2) If the team burn down chart is above the planned burn down line, this indicates that the team will complete the sprint as scheduled.

A. 1) only

B. 2) only

C. Both 1) and 2)

D. Neither 1) nor 2)

6.4.3 Information Radiators

One major communication limitation is that the result is not readily available (Koch, 2005). For example, the result of face-to-face communication is stored in our memory, which may not last long. Written documents filed away in a cabinet may never be seen again. Even files in a computer may not be easily found (do you remember the file name for your last homework assignment?). Even if a file in the computer is easy to find, you may not open it every day. "Information radiator" in agile was invented to solve this problem.

Information radiator is a low-tech metric used in agile software development. It keeps all useful information posted around the team's physical workspace so that they will see it on a regular basis. It is persistent and will be there at all times. It is up to date and reflects the team's current status. It is easy to locate when a member needs it. It is simple to use, since one just raises their head to see the team's progress. In short, the information radiator provides a simple and effective way for any stakeholder to understand the exact status of the development project.

The radiator also helps reinforce important philosophies and principles among the team members. Like TV commercials that are on screen all the time, the radiator can affect team subconscious with information that promotes team morale. Teams can decide what to post and how often to update the posts.

Test Your Understanding 6.29
Information posted around a team's physical working space is called a(n) _____.
A. valuable data
B. team domain
C. information posted
D. information radiator

Test Your Understanding 6.30
An information radiator can help _____.
A. enhance team moral
B. room temperature
C. information flow
D. information distribution

Test Your Understanding 6.31
Information radiators were invented to solve a major limitation of communication. What was the limitation?
A. Not everyone in an agile team spoke English
B. Not everyone had a computer open at all time
C. The result of communication was not readily available
D. The result of communication was not signed by a manager

6.5 Chapter Summary

In this chapter, you learn that if two or more classes have common members (fields and methods), a super class can be created to include those common members and allow other classes to inherit the super class and add their own unique members. This is not just to save typing time. It is one of the most important aspects of object-oriented programming.

In class inheritance, if different sub classes have different implementations of the same method, then you can use abstract classes. An abstract method can be used in the super class. An abstract method has a method header only without a body part.

Similar to an abstract class, an interface can be used to define behaviors for a group of classes as long as they all implement the interface. All interface members are public and abstract by default. You also learned the common communication techniques used in agile. They are the Kanban board, burn down chart, and information radiator. These are just some techniques for you to start with. In the real world, you may modify and enhance them for your own team.

6.6 References:

Broadus III, W. A. (2013). Stakeholder Needs and Expectations: Planning Your Agile Project and Program Metrics. Defense AT & L. Vol.42, Issue 6, Nov/Dec, p 50-54.

Dinsmore, P. C., & Cabanis-Brewin, J. (2014). The AMA Handbook of Project Management. New York: AMACOM.

Koch, A. S. (2005). Agile Software Development : Evaluating the Methods for Your Organization. Boston, MA: Artech House, Inc.

Ordysinski, T. (2013). Kanban Based Information Management in Organization, Studies & Proceedings Polish Association for Knowledge Management, 63, p. 76-85.

Tilk, D. (2016). Five Steps to Agile Project Success, Internal Auditor. Apr. Vol. 73 Issue 2, p57-61.

Vanderjack, B. (2015). The Agile Edge : Managing Projects Effectively Using Agile Scrum. New York: Business Expert Press.

6.7 Solutions to Test Your Understanding:
6.1 A; 6.2 D; 6.3 A; 6.4 C; 6.5 A; 6.6 D; 6.7 B; 6.8 C; 6.9 A; 6.10 A; 6.11 D; 6.12 D; 6.13 C; 6.14 D; 6.15 C; 6.16 A; 6.17 C; 6.18 B; 6.19 A; 6.20 A; 6.21 D; 6.22 C; 6.23 D; 6.24 D; 6.25A; 6.26 C; 6.27 B; 6.28 A; 6.29 D; 6.30 A; 6.31 C;

Chapter 7: C# Exception Handling and Agile Quality Assurance

7.1 What Is C# Exception?

So far, you focused on learning how to make the code run. It is time for you to learn that having an application that solves business problems is only half of the story. The other half, or perhaps more than half, is quality software.

Example 7.1

Problem:
Write an application that calculates the retail price based on the wholesale price plus mark ups. The program prompts the user for the wholesale price and management markup percentage, then displays the retail price. For example, if the wholesale price is $10.00 and the markup percentage is 45%, then the retail price will be $14.50

Solution:

Create a console app project called Chapter7Example1. Type the code inside the Main() method of the Program class. Your completed code should resemble the following.

```
namespace Chapter7Example1
{
```

```
class Program
{
    static void Main()
    {
        //Prompt user for wholesale price and markup
        Console.WriteLine("Enter Wholesale Price:");
        double wholesalePrice =
            double.Parse(Console.ReadLine()!);
        Console.WriteLine("Enter Markup Percentage:");
        double markupPercentage =
            double.Parse(Console.ReadLine()!);
        // calculate retail price
        double retailPrice = wholesalePrice *
            (1 + markupPercentage / 100);
        // display result
        Console.WriteLine($"Retail Price: {retailPrice:C}");
    }
}
}
```

Explanation:

These statements solve the problem. If a user enters 10 as the wholesale price and 45 for the markup percentage, the console will display $14.50 as the retail price. That's correct. However, if the user enters "ten" for the wholesale price, the program will halt and display the following exception:

Figure 7.1 An exception for Example 7.1

This is an example of a run time error. A FormatException was thrown. You cannot convert "ten" to a double value. It's an error that C# caught (Common Language Runtime (CLR) to be exact), so an exception is thrown. An exception is C#'s response to any programming bug, invalid user input, or external issues (such as a connection to a nonexistent file). An exception is often a built-in class.

The above exception was thrown because of invalid user input. Usually, this type of exception can be fixed by the programmer. You can use C# flow control to make sure that the user enters the correct format. You can use an 'if' statement to accomplish this.

You may notice the ! operator used in Console.Readline(). The postfix ! is the null-forgiving operator. It has no effect at run time. It only affects the compiler's static flow analysis (green underline gone).

Example 7.2

Problem:

Use the 'if' statement to handle the exceptions in Example 7.1. If the user enters a non-numeric value for the wholesale price or percentage, display an error message.

Solution:

Copy Chapter7Example1 project folder. Rename it to Chapter7Example2. Open the new project in Visual Studio, Modify the Main method so it looks like:

```
//declare variables to hold user values
double wholesalePrice;
double markupPercentage;
// prompt user for wholesale price
Console.WriteLine("Enter Wholesale Price:");
if(!(double.TryParse(Console.ReadLine(),
    out wholesalePrice)))
{
    Console.WriteLine("Wholesale price must be numeric.");
}
else
{
    // wholesale price is good
    // prompt for markup
    Console.WriteLine("Enter markup percentage:");
```

```
if(!(double.TryParse(Console.ReadLine(),
    out markupPercentage)))
{
    Console.WriteLine("Markup must be numeric.");
}
else
{
    // markup is good
    // calculate retail price
    double retailPrice = wholesalePrice *
        (1 + markupPercentage / 100);
    // display result
    Console.WriteLine($"Retail price: {retailPrice:C}");
}
```

Explanation:

The TryParse() method converts the first argument (what the user enters) to the second argument (the wholesalePrice variable). If the conversion succeeds, the TryParse() method will return true. Otherwise, it will return false. The ! operator is NOT in logic, so if the conversion failed, the condition in the if statement is true (thanks to !). It will then display to the user the feedback, "Wholesale price must be numeric."

You can think of the TryParse() method as doing two things: 1. Converting the first argument to the second argument; 2. Returning true if the conversion is successful, or false if otherwise.

Note that the TryParse() method uses the modifier out for the second parameter. This is because a method can only return one value or reference without using the "out" parameter modifier (see Chapter 4 for more details). You want this method to return two values, one Boolean value and one wholesale price.

An almost identical validation for the markup percentage is nested inside the else block.

Test Your Understanding 7.1
Which of the following statements about exception is correct?
1) An exception is C#'s response to a programming error.
2) An exception is the same as a programming bug.
A. 1) only
B. 2) only
C. Both 1) and 2)
D. Neither 1) nor 2)

Test Your Understanding 7.2
Which of the following statements about exceptions is correct?
1) An exception in C# is a class.
2) If an invalid user input is not handled in the code, it can cause an exception.
A. 1) only
B. 2) only
C. Both 1) and 2)
D. Neither 1) nor 2)

Test Your Understanding 7.3
Which of the following is a C# built-in exception class? This exception will be thrown when the user enters 'ten' when the application expects the number '10'.
A. UserInputException
B. FormatException
C. RuntimeErrorException
D. Number10Exception

Test Your Understanding 7.4
What are the two things the TryParse() method does?
A. Returning two values to the caller.
B. Accepting one value and returning a bool value.
C. Accepting two values and returning a bool value.
D. Passing a value from the first parameter to the second and returning a bool value.

Programming Challenge 7.1
Modify the program in Example 7.2 so that it also won't accept a negative number for the wholesale price nor for the markup percentage.

Example 7.3

Problem:

Example 7.2 fixed the exception issues with the if statements and TryParse() method. However, the user does not get a chance to enter a correct value. Rewrite the program so that the application keeps prompting the user for a value until a value in the correct format is entered.

Analysis:

This program will prompt the user to enter a numeric value for the wholesale price. If a value with an incorrect format is entered, it will prompt again. This is a loop, repeating the prompt until a value in the correct format is entered. Since you don't know how many times the user will enter a value in the wrong format, a while loop fits the purpose well. In short, when the user enters a value in the wrong format, a feedback message is shown and the prompt for entering the data is displayed again until the user enters the data in correct format.

Solution:

Create a console app called Chapter7Example3. Replace the default code in Program.cs with the following:

```csharp
namespace Chapter7Example3
{
    class Program
    {
        static void Main()
        {
            // declare variables to hold user values
            double wholesalePrice;
            double markupPercentage;
            //Prompt user for wholesale price and markup
            Console.WriteLine("Enter Wholesale Price:");
            while (!double.TryParse(Console.ReadLine(),
                out wholesalePrice)
                || (wholesalePrice < 0))
            {
                Console.WriteLine("Wholesale price" +
                    " must be numeric and positive.");
            }
            // wholesalePrice is valid
            Console.WriteLine("Enter markup percentage:");
            while (!double.TryParse(Console.ReadLine(),
                out markupPercentage)
                || markupPercentage < 0)
            {
                Console.WriteLine("Markup must be" +
                    " numeric and positive.");
            }
            // markup percentage is valid
            // calculate retail price
            double retailPrice = wholesalePrice *
                (1 + markupPercentage / 100);
            // display result
            Console.WriteLine($"Retail Price: {retailPrice:C}");
```

```
        }
    }
  }
}
```

Explanation:

Each while loop in the Main() method does only two things: 1) Give feedback to the user, and 2) Receive new input from the user.

The condition for the loop is that the value entered cannot be converted to a double type number 'or' (the || symbol in the code) nor a negative number. As long as one of these two conditions is true, the input is invalid and the loop continues.

Test Your Understanding 7.5
The double.TryParse() method converts a _____ value to a _____ and returns a _____ value.
A. double, string, bool
B. string, double, bool
C. double, bool, string
D. string, bool, double

Programming Challenge 7.2
Write a console application that lets the user enter a student name and an integer score between 0 and 100. Then the application displays the student name and the letter grade by using the formula: 90 or above A; between 80 and 89 B; between 70 and 79 C; between 60 and 69 D; below 60 F.
If the user enters an invalid score, prompt the user to enter again until a valid score is entered.

7.2 Exception Handling with Try ... Catch Statement

Example 7.4

Problem:

Write a console app that asks the user to enter two whole numbers then divides the first number by the second number and displays the quotient.

Analysis:

You can use the same technique in the previous example so that only valid data is accepted. This example uses a different approach. Use the C# built in Exception classes to catch different types of exceptions. Note that in the real world, you should write more robust code to remove the bugs and validate user input. The Exception classes should be used to handle external errors that are rare and unexpected.

Solution 1:

This first solution will not include any exception handling.

Create a project called Chapter7Example4. Replace the default code in Program.cs with the following:

```csharp
namespace Chapter7Example4
{
    class Program
    {
        static void Main()
        {
            // prompt use for dividend
            Console.WriteLine("Enter dividend:");
            int dividend = int.Parse(Console.ReadLine());
            // prompt user for divisor
            Console.WriteLine("Enter divisor:");
            int divisor = int.Parse(Console.ReadLine());
            // calculate the quotient
            int quotient = dividend / divisor;
            // display the result
            Console.WriteLine($"{dividend} divided" +
                $" by {divisor} is {quotient}");
        }
    }
}
```

Explanation:

This program will run if the user enters all valid input. For example, if you enter 10 for dividend and enter 3 for divisor, you will get the correct quotient.

Now try this:

Run the program by entering 5.4 as the dividend. You will see "FormatException"

Next, run the program by entering 5 as the dividend and 0 as the divisor. You will see "DivideByZeroException".

Finally, run the program by entering 2345678901. You will see "OverflowException." This is because the largest int allowed is 2,147,483,647, and you just entered a whole number larger than that.

C# programming has many built in Exception classes. Figure 7.2 shows a small part of the tree in the UML class diagram. All built in exceptions are inherited from the "SystemException" class, which in turn is inherited from the Exception class. All custom build exception classes should inherit from the "ApplicationException" class, which in turn is inherited from the Exception class. The arrows in Figure 7.2 point from a sub class to the super class.

There are many more built-in exception classes under the "SystemException" class. For a complete list, visit https://msdn.microsoft.com/en-us/library/z4c5tckx%28v=vs.110%29.aspx.

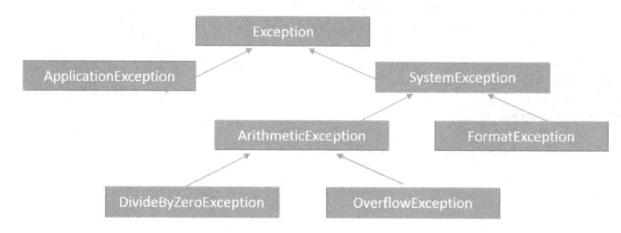

Figure 7.2 Sample built-in exception classes.

Test Your Understanding 7.6
If you want to write a custom exception class, it should be inherited from the _____ class.
A. Exception
B. ApplicationException
C. SystemException
D. CustomException
Test Your Understanding 7.7
In the UML class diagram, an arrow points from ClassA to ClassB, indicating _____.
A. ClassA is a super class
B. ClassB is a super class
C. neither ClassA nor ClassB is a super class

D. both ClassA and ClassB are super classes

Test Your Understanding 7.8
Which of the following is NOT a built-in exception class in C#?
A. Exception
B. ApplicationException
C. SystemException
D. BuiltInException

Test Your Understanding 7.9
If a user enters 2345678901 when an int data type value is expected by the program, what type of exception will it throw?
A. ApplicationException
B. FormatException
C. OverflowException
D. DivideByZeroException

Solution 2:

The second solution to the problem is to use the Try ... Catch statement to handle the exceptions. The following code shows the solution for Example 7.4 written with the Try ... Catch statement:

```csharp
namespace Chapter7Example4
{
    class Program
    {
        static void Main()
        {
            try
            {
                // prompt use for dividend
                Console.WriteLine("Enter dividend:");
                int dividend = int.Parse(Console.ReadLine());
                // prompt user for divisor
                Console.WriteLine("Enter divisor:");
                int divisor = int.Parse(Console.ReadLine());
                // calculate the quotient
                int quotient = dividend / divisor;
                // display the result
                Console.WriteLine($"{dividend} divided" +
                    $" by {divisor} is {quotient}");
            }
```

```csharp
        catch (DivideByZeroException ex)
        {
            Console.WriteLine(ex.Message);
        }
        catch (OverflowException ex)
        {
            Console.WriteLine(ex.Message);
        }
        catch (ArithmeticException ex)
        {
            Console.WriteLine(ex.Message);
        }
        catch (FormatException ex)
        {
            Console.WriteLine(ex.Message);
        }
        catch (SystemException ex)
        {
            Console.WriteLine(ex.Message);
        }
        catch (Exception ex)
        {
            Console.WriteLine(ex.Message);
        }

        finally
        {
            Console.WriteLine("Thank you!");
        }
    }
  }
}
```

Explanation:

You put all the statements that may throw an exception inside the try block. When an exception is thrown, the execution will jump to one of the catch blocks and end up in the finally block.

You may notice how the sequence of catch blocks is organized. All catch blocks should be organized from specific to general, with more specific exceptions first and more general exceptions later.

By examining the class diagram in Figure 7.2, you can see a super class is more general and a sub class is more specific. This is because when one exception is caught, the program will leave the Try... Catch statement (and go to the finally block if it exists). If you put the most general exception class first, it will catch any exception and leave the statement and make the rest of the catch blocks useless.

After the execution of either the try or catch block, the finally block will follow. The "finally" block is optional.

Test Your Understanding 7.10
Which of the following statements about try ... catch is correct?
1) When using the try ... catch statement to handle the exception, only one catch block will be executed at most, even if you put multiple catch blocks in the application.
2) When using the try ... catch ... finally statement, the finally block will always be executed whether an exception is thrown or not.
A. 1) only
B. 2) only
C. Both 1) and 2)
D. Neither 1) nor 2)

Test Your Understanding 7.11
When using the try ... catch statement to handle the exception, in the catch blocks, you should put more _____ exception classes before the more _____ exception classes.
A. general, specific
B. specific, general
C. frequent, rare
D. rare, frequent

Programming Challenge 7.3
Write an application that can calculate a trip's gas usage in miles per gallon. The application prompts the user for the number of miles of a trip and how many gallons of gas was used for the trip. Then the application should display the miles per gallon. Use the try ... catch ... finally to handle the exceptions.

7.3 Software Quality

Quality is in the eyes of the beholder. Different people see the same software with differing levels of quality. Even the same person may see the same software at different times with differing quality. Furthermore, the definition of software quality may be different among experts. We believe that quality is about fulfilling requirements (Marchewka, 2015).

To understand quality, you need to know the eight characteristics of software quality defined by ISO/IEC 25010 (2011):

1. Functional suitability: A high quality application should meet the stated and implied needs of the users.

2. Performance efficiency: A high quality application should not require too many resources.

3. Compatibility: A high quality application should be able to exchange information with other applications easily.

4. Usability: A high quality application can be used by specified users for specific goals.

5. Reliability: A high quality application should perform specified functions under specified conditions for a long time without problems.

6. Security: A high quality application should provide protections for its information and data.

7. Maintainability: A high quality application should allow effective and efficient modifications when needed.

8. Portability: A high quality application can be easily transferred from one environment to another.

Test Your Understanding 7.12
There is more than one definition of quality. Which of the following is the definition from this book?
A. Quality is in the eyes of the beholder.
B. There is no definition for quality.
C. Quality is about fulfilling requirements.
D. Quality is something that will last forever.

Test Your Understanding 7.13
'A high-quality application should meet the stated and implied needs of the users' describes which characteristic of software quality according to ISO/IEC 25010?
A. Functional suitability
B. Performance efficiency
C. Compatibility
D. Usability

Test Your Understanding 7.14
'A high-quality application should not require too many resources' describes which characteristic of software quality by ISO/IEC 25010?
A. Functional suitability
B. Performance efficiency
C. Compatibility
D. Usability

Test Your Understanding 7.15

'A high-quality application can be used by specified users for specified goals' describes which characteristic of software quality by ISO/IEC 25010?
A. Functional suitability
B. Performance efficiency
C. Compatibility
D. Usability

Test Your Understanding 7.16
'A high quality application should allow modifications when needed in an effective and efficient way' describes which characteristic of software quality by ISO/IEC 25010?
A. Reliability
B. Security
C. Maintainability
D. Portability

Test Your Understanding 7.17
'A high-quality application should perform specified functions under specified conditions for a long time without problems' describes which characteristic of software quality by ISO/IEC 25010?
A. Reliability
B. Security
C. Maintainability
D. Portability

Test Your Understanding 7.18
Which of the following is NOT a characteristic of software quality defined by ISO/IEC 25010?
A. Functional suitability
B. Performance efficiency
C. Compatibility
D. Developer reputation

Test Your Understanding 7.19
Which of the following is NOT a characteristic of software quality defined by ISO/IEC 25010?
A. Usability
B. Reliability
C. Reusability
D. Security

7.4 Quality Philosophies and Principles

Software quality depends a lot on the development team. There are four general philosophies and principles that can guide a team through its journey in software development (Marchewka, 2015).

1. Focus on customer satisfaction: Software development is not to show off how smart the team is. It is to satisfy the customers' requirements. Only when this philosophy is a part of the team norm can the agile principles be implemented. Another reason for meeting customer and stakeholder requirements is because the customer is the ultimate judge of the quality (Ginac, 1998).

2. Prevention, Not Inspection: The cost of quality depends on its four components —prevention, inspection, internal failure, and external failure. The most efficient way to reduce the quality cost is through prevention (Lewis, 2008). The business rule of ten can be applied here. When a quality issue is identified by a team member, the cost may be $1. When the same issue is noticed by a customer, the cost can be $10.

3. Quality Is Everyone's Responsibility: Quality is not free. It requires time and effort. Team members should be responsible and empowered for ensuring quality and encouraged to take pride in their work. Every member should commit to the quality (McKay, 2007; Jyothi and Rao, 2012).

4. Fact-Based Management: Numbers, pictures, and charts should be used for ease of understanding and quick references. Data collected can be used for evaluating and improving the process (Kloppenborg and Petrick. 2002).

Test Your Understanding 7.20
'The goal of software development is to satisfy the customers' requirements' describes which quality philosophy?
A. Fact-Based Management
B. Focus on customer satisfaction
C. Prevention, not inspection
D. Quality is everyone's responsibility

Test Your Understanding 7.21
'Team members should be responsible and empowered for ensuring quality and encouraged to take pride in their work' describes which quality philosophy?
A. Fact-Based Management
B. Focus on customer satisfaction
C. Prevention, not inspection
D. Quality is everyone's responsibility

Test Your Understanding 7.22
Which of the following is NOT a quality philosophy discussed in the book?
A. Quality is not tangible
B. Focus on customer satisfaction
C. Prevention, not inspection
D. Quality is everyone's responsibility

7.5 Pair Programming

As you learned in Chapter 1, a non-agile team typically has a very clear line between the roles of developer and quality assurance (QA). This can be a problem.

Let's use an example. A developer is working on feature A and a QA may be working on something else. After the developer completes feature A and moves on to Feature B, the QA will start to test on feature A and may find some bugs. Now the developer has to stop working on feature B, reset up the environment for working on feature A, and fix the bugs of feature A. This will repeat for every feature, making the process inefficient and of low quality.

The pair programming approach will start with both the developer and the QA working on the test case before the developer starts coding. This will help the developer better understand the case and write better code. Once the developer starts to code, the QA can follow with the testing. This kind of teamwork ensures higher quality with less time spent on setting up the environment.

In short, agile requires a cross functional team which means the developer understands how the QA works, and the QA knows the programming. They should both know the analysis and design. By physically sitting together and working together, they can test the code as it is written. This increases the quality of software.

Pair programming involves two team members working on one computer with just one keyboard and mouse. The member who works at the keyboard with the mouse is called the "driver", and the other member who is also actively participating in the current work is called the "navigator". The two members take turns controlling the keyboard and mouse.

Pair programming allows team members with different expertise to code together, take turns controlling the keyboard, and learning from each other (Beck and Andres, 2005). There can be different flavors of pair programming. For example, peer review or peer code review is similar to pair programming.

Researchers have identified many benefits of pair programming (Hannay, 2009; Vanhanen and Mantyla, 2013). Improved quality is at the top of the list. Pair programming can result in higher quality products due to team effort. Also, "programming out loud" helps programmers think more clearly about the requirements.

When a development team is not physically located in one place, communication and collaboration may be more difficult and can negatively impact the performance of the pair programming. There are positive reports that benefits are still possible in the virtual team, even in the asynchronous mode (Zin, 2006). Carefully selected communication tools that are comfortable to use for all participants and sufficient training of team members will minimize the failure of pair programming in a distributed environment (Canfora et al, 2006).

Test Your Understanding 7.23
Which of the following statements about pair programming is correct?
1) Pair programming works with two team members working together on one computer with two sets of keyboard and mouse.
2) Pair programming helps programmers think more clearly about the requirements.
A. 1) only
B. 2) only
C. Both 1) and 2)
D. Neither 1) nor 2)

Test Your Understanding 7.24
In pair programming, the member who works at the keyboard with the mouse is called the _____.
A. navigator
B. warrior
C. active coder
D. driver

Test Your Understanding 7.25

In pair programming, the member who is away from the keyboard and the mouse is called the
_____.
A. navigator
B. warrior
C. active coder
D. driver

Test Your Understanding 7.26
According to the author of this book, which of the following statements about pair programming is correct?
1) Pair programming allows team members to learn from each other.
2) The only concern of pair programming is the efficiency with two members working on one task.
A. 1) only
B. 2) only
C. Both 1) and 2)
D. Neither 1) nor 2)

7.6 Test Driven Development (TDD):

In traditional testing, the developers first write the code and testers test it afterwards. TDD requires that developers first write automated test cases and then write only the code necessary to make the test cases pass with no issues. This encourages the developers to think through the requirements before writing the code, encourages only the code that is needed is written, and ensures that each piece of the code has gone through an initial quality check before formal testing.

Example 7.5
Problem:
Write a test case so that if a student's test score is 70 or above, then the student's final grade is "Pass".

Solution:
Start a console app called Chapter7Example5. Open Program.cs in the code view. Replace the default code with the following:

```
namespace Chapter7Example5
{
    public class Program
```

```
{
   static void Main()
   {
   }
}
}
```

In the "Solution Explorer" window, right click on the Solution (not project, as you did so far to add a class to the project), then "Add" and "New Project" as shown in Figure 7.3.

Figure 7.3 Add a new project to the Solution.

In the "Add a new project" dialog box, search "C# MSTest", then select "MSTest Test Project". Click on the "Next" button to continue (Figure 7.4 button not shown).

Figure 7.4 Add New Project of UnitTest Dialog box

In the "Configure your new project" dialogue box, just accept the default project name. Click on the "Next" button to continue.

In the "Additional Information" dialogue box, click on the "Create" button to create the project. The new code window will have the "UnitTest1.cs" open as shown in Figure 7.5.

```csharp
using Microsoft.VisualStudio.TestTools.UnitTesting;

namespace TestProject1
{
    [TestClass]
    0 references
    public class UnitTest1
    {
        [TestMethod]
        0 references
        public void TestMethod1()
        {
        }
    }
}
```

Figure 7.5 Default UnitTest1.cs file code

Now add the following statements inside the "TestMethod1()" method:

```
// create an object to test
Student student = new Student();
// define a test input and output value
int score = 70;
string expectedResult = "Pass";
// run the method under test
string actualResult = student.ShowPassFail(score);
// verify the result
Assert.AreEqual(expectedResult, actualResult);
```

The Student class has a red squiggle underscore, which is ok, because a class called Student has not been created yet.

Next, you will generate the Student class and the corresponding method from the test.

Place the cursor on the red squiggle beneath Student, Note the yellow light bulb. Click on the dropdown. On the shortcut menu, choose "Generate new type…" (Figure 7.6).

Figure 7.6 Code with shortcut menu

The "Generate Type" dialog box will popup. Set Project to the "Chapter7Example5" project. Select the "create new file" radio button, then click on "OK", as shown in Figure 7.7.

Figure 7.7 Generate Type Dialog box.

You should see the red squiggle under Student disappear. The ShowPassFail() method now has a red squiggle underscore. Next, place the cursor on ShowPassFail(). The light bulb will appear (alternatively, you can right click on the method and select "Quick Action" in the context menu). Click the dropdown on the light bulb. On the shortcut menu, choose the "Generate method" stub (Figure 7.8). You should see the red squiggle disappeared.

```csharp
// create an object to test
Student student = new Student();
// define a test input and output value
int score = 70;
string expectedResult = "Pass";
// run the method under test
string actualResult = student.ShowPassFail(score);
// verify the result
Assert.AreEqual(expectedRes  Generate method 'Student.ShowPassFail'
```

Figure 7.8 Light bulb with Generate method

It's time for running the unit test.

On the "Test" menu, choose "Run All Tests" as shown in Figure 7.9.

Figure 7.9 Run test menu

The solution builds and runs. (This may take a few seconds). The "Test Explorer" window opens and displays the results. The test appears under Failed Tests as shown in Figure 7.10. The test failed because you don't have the code for the ShowPassFail() yet.

Figure 7.10 Text Explorer window

You just completed a test case. It's time to develop the code.

Open the "Student.cs" in the code window, and replace the default code inside the ShowPassFail:

```
string passFail="Fail";
if (score == 70)
{
    passFail = "Pass";
}
return passFail;
```

Save and run the test again. You should see the success in the "Test Explorer" window (Figure 7.11).

Figure 7.11 Test passed.

You may notice one problem in the example so far. What if the score is 71? Will it still be a "Pass"?

No. Something is wrong with the test case. Let's add a new TestMethod() with the code below:

```
[TestMethod]
public void TestMethod2()
{
    // create an object to test
    Student student = new Student();
    // define a test input and output value
    for(int score = 70; score <= 100; score++)
    {
        string expectedResult = "Pass";
        // run the method under test
        string actualResult = student.ShowPassFail(score);
        // verify the result
        Assert.AreEqual(expectedResult, actualResult);
    }
}
```

Explanation:

While TestMethod1() tests for just one case: when the score is 70, TestMethod2() tests for all possible scores between 70 and 100 with a for loop.

Now run the test. TestMethod1 will pass, but TestMethod2 will fail, as shown in Figure 7.12

Figure 7.12 Test Explorer window with TestMethod1 passed, but TestMethod2 failed.

Go back to the Student class. Change the equal sign in the following line to a greater than or equal to sign:

    if (score == 70)

To

    if (score >= 70)

Save and run all tests again. You should see both TestMethods passed, as shown in Figure 7.13

Figure 7.13 Test Explorer window indicates both testmethods passed

Test Your Understanding 7.27
Which of the following statements about code testing is correct?
1) In agile, the developers must first write the code. Testers test it afterwards.
2) In test driven development, you write a test case before you write software code.
A. 1) only
B. 2) only
C. Both 1) and 2)
D. Neither 1) nor 2)

Test Your Understanding 7.28
Which of the following statements about TDD is correct?
1) In test driven development, you only write enough software code to make it pass the test.
2) In test methods, a for loop is often used to test multiple cases.
A. 1) only
B. 2) only
C. Both 1) and 2)
D. Neither 1) nor 2)

7.7 Chapter Summary

In this chapter, you learned exception handling in C#. One way to handle the exception is to write more robust code, such as using the 'if' statement. Another way is to use the Try ... Catch statement with the built-in exception classes.

You also learned software quality and how agile enhances the quality of the software developed. You learned how pair programming works and how it enhances the software quality. Finally, you got hands-on experience with test-driven-development (TDD).

7.8 References

Beck, K. and Andres, C. (2005), Extreme Programming Explained: Embrace Change, 2nd Edition, Addison-Wesley.

Canfora, G., Cimitile, A., Di Lucca, G. A., Visaggio, C. A. (2006). How Distribution Affects the Success of Pair Programming. INTERNATIONAL JOURNAL OF SOFTWARE ENGINEERING & KNOWLEDGE ENGINEERING. April Vol. 16 Issue 2, p293-313

Ginac, F. P. (1998), Customer Oriented Software Qual- ity Assurance. Upper Saddle River, NJ: Prentice Hall.

Hannay, J. E., Dyba, T., Arisholm, E., and Sjoberg, D. I. K. (2009). The Effectiveness of Pair Programming: A Meta Analysis. *Information and Software Technology.* 51(7). July, p. 1110-1122.

ISO/IEC 25010:2011(en), Systems and software engineering — Systems and software Quality Requirements and Evaluation (SQuaRE) — System and software quality models. Available at: https://www.iso.org/obp/ui/#iso:std:iso-iec:25010:ed-1:v1:en visited November 22, 2016.

Jyothi, V.E. and Rao, K. N. (2012). Effective Implementation of Agile Practices - Incoordination with Lean Kanban, International Journal on Computer Science and Engineering, 4(1), p. 87-91.

Kloppenborg, T. J. and J. A. Petrick. (2002), Managing Project Quality. Vienna, VA: Management Concepts.

Lewis, W. E. (2008), Software Testing and Continuous Quality Improvement. 3rd Edition, Boca Raton, FL: Auer- bach.

Marchewka, J. T. (2015), *Information Technology Project Management*, 5th Edition. Wiley.

McKay, J. (2007), "Quality Just Doesn't Happen." CIO Magazine. May 24.

Vanhanen, J. and Mantyla, M. V. (2013). A Systematic Mapping Study of Empirical Studies on the Use of Pair Programming in Industry, International Journal of Software Engineering and Knowledge Engineering, Vol. 23, Issue 9, p. 1221-1267.

Zin, A. M. Idris, S., and Subramaniam, N. K. (2006). Implementing Virtual Pair Programming in E-Learning Environment, JOURNAL OF INFORMATION SYSTEMS EDUCATION. Summer, Vol. 17 Issue 2, p113-117.

7.9 Solutions to Test Your Understanding

7.1 A; 7.2 C; 7.3 B; 7.4 D; 7.5 B; 7.6 B; 7.7 B; 7.8 D; 7.9 C; 7.10 C; 7.11 B; 7.12 C; 7.13 A; 7.14 B; 7.15 D; 7.16 C; 7.17 A; 7.18 D; 7.19 C; 7.20 B; 7.21 D; 7.22 A; 7.23 B; 7.24 D; 7.25 A; 7.26 A; 7.27 B; 7.28 C;

Chapter 8: C# Windows Forms Application and Agile Summary

8.1 Windows Forms Application

You have learned basic object-oriented programming in C# from previous chapters. It's time to use that knowledge to build some Graphical User Interface (GUI) desktop applications.

Example 8.1

Problem:

The Tiny College needs an application that allows instructors to enter student IDs, student names, and numeric test scores between 0 and 100 for the semester. They want these data to be saved in a text file that can be pulled out, displayed, and printed as wanted.

User Stories:

Based on the description and talking to some employees at The Tiny College, you come up with the following user stories.

User Story 1: As an instructor, I want to save my student's ID, name, and score in a text file so that I can keep student's records.

Acceptance Criteria: Graphical user interface. A score is a whole number between 0 and 100.

User Story 2: As an administrator, I want to see all students' records in one screen with student ID, student name, and corresponding letter grades so that I can have an overall picture of my college.

Acceptance Criteria: Graphical user interface. All students listed on one screen. Letter grade is based on the formula: 90-100 A; 80-89 B; 70-79 C; 60-69 D; Under 60 F.

User Story 3: As a staff member, I want to be able to search a particular student by student ID so that I can decide if the student is qualified for registration.

Acceptance Criteria: Graphical user interface. When the student ID is entered, only that student's name and letter grade are shown. The letter grade formula is the same as in story 2. The Tiny College requires all students to have a grade of C or higher to qualify for registration.

User Story 4: As a user of the application, I want to be able to print the student record from the application so that I can give it to the students or for the convenience of discussion with the students.

Acceptance Criteria: Graphical user interface. The administrator wants to print all records in one document with appropriate headers and date time of printing. The staff wants to print just one student record.

Solution:

Start Visual Studio. Create a new "Project" as you did in the past, but don't use "Console Application" as you've used in the previous chapters. This time, on the "Create a new project" window, select "Windows Forms App" as shown in Figure 8.1 and click on the "next" button.

Windows Forms App

A project template for creating a .NET Windows Forms (WinForms) App.

    C#   Windows   Desktop

Figure 8.1 Select "Windows Forms App.

On the "Configure your new project" window, name the project "Chapter8Example1". Make sure the "Place solution and project in the same directory" checkbox is checked. Click on the "Next" button to move to the "Additional Information" window. Make sure ".NET 6.0(Long-term support) is selected for framework. Click on the "Create" button to start a new blank window form application. It may take a couple of minutes for the form to show in design view (double click on the Form1.cs in Solution Explorer window if necessary).

As you continue to develop the application, pay special attention to the following terms: design view window, controls and toolbox, properties window, solution explorer window, and code window.

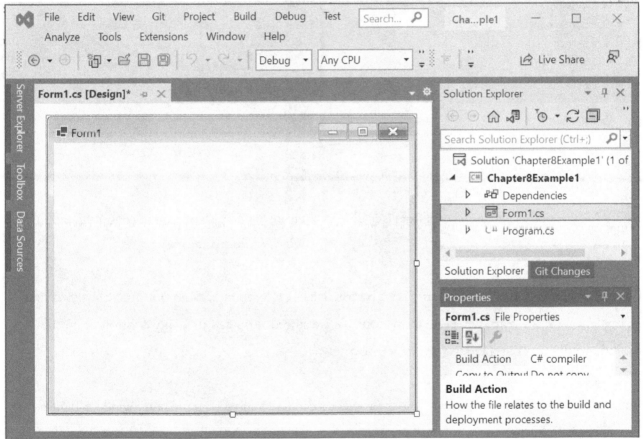

Figure 8.2 Design View Window

Design view window is a Windows form you use during design. Whatever you put on it will be shown when ran. Figure 8.2 is the design view window. You can add controls, such as a button, to the form.

To find the toolbox, click on the "Toolbox" tab on the left side. Or "View" on the menu, then "toolbox". Controls are organized by categories (Figure 8.3). Expand a category by clicking on it (Figure 8.4). If you want to add a control to the form, you should open the form in the design view. Just double click on an item in the toolbox you want to add to the form, or drag and drop the control to the form.

Figure 8.3 Toolbox categories when a form is in design view.

Figure 8.4 A small portion of controls in the All Windows Forms category.

Controls are object items on a form, like a button, a label, a textbox, a radio button, a checkbox and so on. Toolbox is a place where all those controls are stored. You can drag any controls from the toolbox to the form in the design view window.

Each control has many properties. Those properties can be found in the property window(Figure 8.2). For example, a button has the "text" property, which will be the text shown on the button.

Solution Explorer Window is the same one you see throughout the book. All the files of the project can be found there.

Every form has a design view (explained above) and a code view. The design view helps you design the look of a form while the code view allows you to enter code and makes the form interactive.

Next, let us rename the default Form1.cs file in the project to something more meaningful. In the "Solution Explorer" window, right click on the Form1.cs. Select "Rename" as shown in Figure 8.5.

Figure 8.5 Rename Form1.cs

Change the Form1 name to MainForm.cs (No space in the name). A popup will be displayed asking if you want to change the name for all corresponding components (Figure 8.6). Click yes.

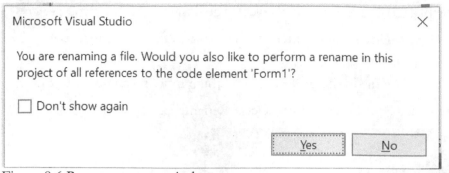

Figure 8.6 Rename popup window

Next, make the title/caption of the MainForm more readable instead of using the default "Form1". First, click (do not double click) on anywhere in the form to select it. You should see the "Properties" window (Bottom right corner in Figure 8.2). If you don't see it, you can right click on the form and then select "Properties". By default, the properties are organized by category. You can click on the "A to Z alphabetical" icon (second from left) to see a different organization.

Figure 8.7 The properties window.

Find the "Text" property in the properties window (Figure 8.7). Change its default value from

"Form1" to "Main Form" (note the use of space between words for users). If the "Text" property is not shown, you may scroll down the list.

Test Your Understanding 8.1
Every Windows form in the develop environment has a _____ view and a _____ view
A. design, code
B. user, design
C. code, user
D. developer, user

Test Your Understanding 8.2
A text field you want to add to a form is called a _____.
A. design item
B. user item
C. control
D. property

Test Your Understanding 8.3
Where can you find all the controls you can add to a form in a design view?
A. design view
B. Solution Explorer
C. Properties Window
D. toolbox

Test Your Understanding 8.4
If you want to change the settings of a control, such as the title/caption of a form, where can you find those settings?
A. design view
B. Solution Explorer
C. Properties Window
D. toolbox

Test Your Understanding 8.5
If you want to change the title/caption of a form, what property of the form would you change?
A. Title
B. Caption
C. either Title or Caption
D. Text

8.2 Add Controls to the Form

In this section, you will learn how to add different controls to a Windows form.

With the MainForm displayed in the designer window, go to the "Toolbox". Add a label control to the form, then click once on the label in the form to select it (if it is not already selected by default). Go to the properties window, change the "Text" property to "Student Records", then find the "Font" property and click once to select it. Click on the ellipsis button (small button with little dots, Figure 8.8) on the right to open the font dialogue window.

Figure 8.8 Properties window with the Font property displayed

In the font dialog box, select the font, style, and size of your liking. In Figure 8.9, the selected font is "Lucida Handwriting", font style is "Italic", and the size is 24.

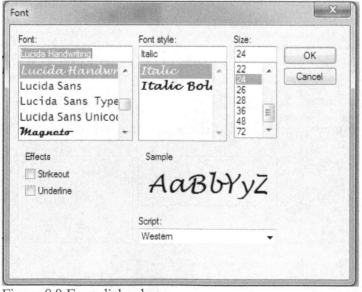

Figure 8.9 Font dialog box

Next, add four buttons to the form. Make the property of each button according to the values in Table 8.1 (the & sign in front of a character makes the quick key at run time where a user press Alt+character-key on keyboard to click the button):

Click once to select	Change "Text" property to	Change "Name" property to
Button1	&Add	addButton
Button2	&Display	displayButton
Button3	&Search	searchButton
Button4	E&xit	exitButton

Table 8.1 Properties for the Main Form buttons.

Figure 8.10 The MainForm with the controls

8.3 Add Event Handler to a Button

In previous chapters of the book, you learned the flow of code execution follows one of three ways: 1. sequential, 2) conditional, and 3) repeating. In this section, you will learn another way. A Windows Form application is event-driven. The flow of the execution of the statements is determined by events such as user actions (e.g. mouse click, key press). In this section, you will write statements to make the buttons on the form work.

Open the main form in the "design view" window by double clicking on "MainForm.cs" in the "Solution Explorer" window, if it is not already open. Then double click on the "Exit" button to create a button click event handler. When the user clicks on this button at run-time, all statements inside the handler will be executed. For now, you just need one statement to exit the application. Add Close(); inside the handler so that the code will look like (You type the bolded line):

```
namespace Chapter8Example1
{
    public partial class MainForm : Form
    {
        public MainForm()
        {
            InitializeComponent();
        }

        private void exitButton_Click(object sender, EventArgs e)
        {
            Close();
        }
    }
}
```

Next, click on the "Save all" icon in Visual Studio to save the project. Then click on the green play button on top to run the application. Your Exit button should work as expected.

Test Your Understanding 8.6
The flow of execution of the statements as determined by events, such as user actions, is called _____ programming.
A. sequential
B. conditional
C. repeating
D. event-driven

Test Your Understanding 8.7
Windows Form application is _____.
A. sequential
B. conditional
C. repeating
D. event-driven

Test Your Understanding 8.8
Which of the following statements about buttons is correct?
1) With the form in the design view, double clicking on a button in the form generates the button click event handler.
2) All statements inside a button click event handler will be executed when the user clicks on the button at run time.
A. 1) only
B. 2) only
C. Both 1) and 2)

D. Neither 1) nor 2)

8.4 Add Student Class to the Project

The application is about students at The Tiny College. You need a class called Student that has three fields (ID, name, and score) and a method (GetLetterGrade()). Go to the "Solution Explorer" window and right click on the "Chapter8Example1" project and add a new class named Student.cs as you did in the previous chapters. Add the following code inside the Student class:

```csharp
// fields
private string studentId;
private string name;
private int score;
// properties
public string StudentId
{
    get { return studentId; }
    set { studentId = value; }
}
public string Name
{
    get { return name; }
    set { name = value; }
}
public int Score
{
    get { return score; }
    set { score = value; }
}
// constructor
public Student(string studentId, string name, int score)
{
    this.studentId = studentId;
    this.name = name;
    this.score = score;
}
// method
public char GetLetterGrade()
{
    char letterGrade;
    if (Score >= 90)
    {
```

```
        letterGrade = 'A';
    }
    else if (Score >= 80)
    {
        letterGrade = 'B';
    }
    else if (Score >= 70)
    {
        letterGrade = 'C';
    }
    else if (Score >= 60)
    {
        letterGrade = 'D';
    }
    else
    {
        letterGrade = 'F';
    }
    return letterGrade;
}
// ToString() method
public override string ToString()
{
    string str;
    str = $"{StudentId}\n{Name}\n{Score}";
    return str;
}
```

Explanation:
The "\n" inside the ToString method indicates "new line". It is the same as pressing the "Enter" key. As a result, the str variable hold text in three lines.

Test Your Understanding 8.9
Which of the following statements about adding a class to the project is correct?
1) Adding a class to a Windows Form project is the same as adding a class to a console project.
2) The project typically appears as the first line in the solution explorer window.
A. 1) only
B. 2) only
C. Both 1) and 2)
D. Neither 1) nor 2)

Test Your Understanding 8.10
What is the "\n" in the following string?
```
string str = $"{StudentId}\n, {Name}\n, {GetLetterGrade()}\n";
```

A. new character
B. new variable
C. new line
D. no more

8.5 User Story 1

User Story 1: As an instructor, I want to save my student's ID, name, and score in a text file so that I can keep student's records.

Acceptance Criteria: Graphical user interface. A score is a whole number between 0 and 100.

The project needs a new form to let an instructor save student records in a text file. Similar to adding a class to a project, in the "Solution Explorer" window, right click on the Chapter8Example1 project, then "Add" and then "Form (Windows Forms)...".

The "Add New Form" dialog box will pop up as shown in Figure 8.11. Name this new form as DataEntryForm.cs. Click on the "Add" button to add this new form.

Figure 8.11 The "Add New Form" Dialog window

Next, have the "Toolbox" window showing. Add the following controls to the Data Entry Form (must be in design view) by double clicking on each control in the toolbox (each double click adds only one control):

1 GroupBox, 3 Labels, 3 TextBoxes, and 3 Buttons.

Reorganize the "Data Entry Form" so the controls look like Figure 8.12. You can move a control by dragging and moving. Note that all controls except the buttons are inside the group box control (Just enlarge the groupbox and drag controls inside it).

With the Data Entry Form in the design view, change its Text property to "Data Entry Form" (note the space between words).

Figure 8.12 Data Entry Form with controls added

Click once on groupBox1, but not on any controls inside the groupBox1, to select it. Go to the "Properties" window and change its "Text" property from "groupBox1" to "Student Data". Click anywhere to save the change. You should see the "groupBox1" on the form change to "Student Data". If a property window does not show, you can right click on the group box and select "Properties".

Follow the same rule: click once on the control, go to the "Properties" window and change its properties listed in Table 8.2. The blank cell means no change is necessary. We don't recommend changing a control name when it is never used in the code. The & character makes the button's quick key. Users can use alt+letter on the keyboard to click on the button instead of using a mouse.

Click once to select	Change "Text" property to	Change "Name" property to
groupBox1	Student Data	
label1	Student ID:	
label2	Student Name:	
label3	Student Score:	
textBox1		idTextBox
textBox2		nameTextBox
textBox3		scoreTextBox
button1	&Save	saveButton
button2	&Clear	clearButton
button3	Cl&ose	closeButton

Table 8.1 Properties for Data Entry Form controls

The completed form should look like Figure 8.13 (name property cannot be seen; make sure you did change them).

Figure 8.13 Data Entry Form with all controls' properties set

Make the close button on the form work by double clicking the "Close" button and add one line of code inside the click event handler:

Close();

To test the app, you need to reopen the MainForm in the design view. Double click on the "Add" button. Add the following two lines inside the button click event handler:

```
DataEntryForm entryForm = new DataEntryForm();
entryForm.ShowDialog();
```

The first line creates an instance of the DataEntryForm class. The second line calls its ShowDialog method to show the form.

Save and run the app. Click on the "Add" button on the main form. The data entry form will show. Click on the "Close" button to close the form. Back to the main form, click on the "Exit" button.

Next, make the "Clear" button on the "Data Entry Form" erase anything the user enters, but not saved on the form. Back in the Designer window of the "Data Entry Form", double click on the "Clear" button to create the "clear button click event handler" and add the following lines inside the "clear button click event handler":

```
idTextBox.Clear();
nameTextBox.Clear();
scoreTextBox.Clear();
idTextBox.Focus();
```

Explanation:

Every control in the toolbox is a class which has built-in methods. For instance, idTextBox is an object you instantiate from the TextBox class which has a method called Clear(). The method will remove any content in the textbox. The Focus() is another method of the TextBox class which will receive the focus of the form (blink cursor).

Save and run the application. You should see that anything typed into the textboxes are gone and the ID field receives the focus once the Clear button is clicked.

The final task in Story 1 is to make the "Save" button work. Back in the designer window of the "Data Entry Form", double click on the "Save" button to create "save button click event handler". Add the following code inside the handler:

```
using StreamWriter sw = File.AppendText("student.txt");
    if (!(string.IsNullOrWhiteSpace(idTextBox.Text) ||
      string.IsNullOrWhiteSpace(nameTextBox.Text) ||
      string.IsNullOrWhiteSpace(scoreTextBox.Text)))
  {
    if (int.TryParse(scoreTextBox.Text, out int score)
       && score >= 0 && score <= 100)
    {
      // make an object from the data entry form
      Student student = new Student
        (idTextBox.Text, nameTextBox.Text, score);
      // save the student record to the file
      sw.WriteLine(student);
      // clear the textboxes
      clearButton.PerformClick();
    }
    else
```

```
    {
        MessageBox.Show("Score must be an integer[0, 100]");
    }
}
else
{
    MessageBox.Show("All fields are required.");
}
```

Explanation:

The following line:

using **StreamWriter sw = File.AppendText**("student.txt");

is a using statement which provides an easy way to open, write, and then close the connection between this application and the text file, and to ensure the correct use of Disposable objects. This line also creates a StreamWriter object named sw which has a WriteLine() method you can use to save text to the file.

The outer if statement checks whether the three textboxes are not empty before saving the contents. A button class has the PerformClick method. It is convenient to call the "clear button click event handler" you wrote earlier and perform the clearance. This provides good user experience as it makes the form ready for the next input.

The else block displays a message to the user if any of the three textboxes are empty.

Save and run the application. Add a few student records.

To see the data you just saved, go to the folder where you saved the project and open the bin folder inside your project, then open the debug folder. Open the net6.0-windows folder. The file with the name student.txt should be inside. You can open it with Notepad or any text editor to view the content.

Test Your Understanding 8.11
A control can be added to a form by _____ clicking on it in the _____. However, you still need to organize it on the form by moving it around.
A. single, toolbox
B. double, toolbox
C. single, form
D. double, form

Test Your Understanding 8.12
Each control has a name property coming with a default value. We recommend that you change it if the control will appear in the _____.
A. form
B. code
C. design view
D. Solution Explorer Window

Test Your Understanding 8.13
How do you add an underscore to a button in a form?
A. use the underscore key on the keyboard
B. click on the underscore icon on the property window
C. add the & in front of the character of the "Text" property
D. add the _ in front of the character of the "Text" property

Test Your Understanding 8.14
Where can you find all the controls to add to a form?
A. Control window
B. Toolbox window
C. Properties window
D. Design View window

Test Your Understanding 8.15
You need to give a meaningful name to a control used in the statements. Where can you change a control's name?
A. Control window
B. Toolbox window
C. Properties window
D. Design View window

Test Your Understanding 8.16
If you want to view or move the controls on the form. Where can you find the form?
A. Control window
B. Toolbox window
C. Properties window
D. Design View window

Test Your Understanding 8.17
Which of the following statements about Windows from is correct?
1) The process of adding a Windows form to a project is the same as adding a class to a project.
2) When you have more than one form in your application, make sure you have a main form that introduces all other forms.
A. 1) only

B. 2) only
C. Both 1) and 2)
D. Neither 1) nor 2)

8.6 User Story 2

User Story 2

As an administrator, I want to see all students' records on one screen with student ID, student name, and corresponding letter grades so that I can see an overall picture of my college.

Acceptance Criteria: Graphical user interface. All students listed on one screen. Letter grade is based on the formula: 90-100 A; 80-89 B; 70-79 C; 60-69 D; Under 60 F.

Analysis:

This story requires that every line of data from the student.txt file be retrieved. Every three lines make a student. You will put every three lines into a student object. Then, you will add the student object into a List and display the List in a Listbox control. All these should happen when the Form loads.

Solution:

Add a new form named DisplayForm to the project. This form will display all student records.

Right click on the project in the "solution explorer" window. Add a Windows Form. When the new form is displayed, go to the Toolbox window and add a label, a listbox and two buttons to the form. Set the properties for each control by using the values in Table 8.3.

Click once to select	Change "Text" property to	Change "Name" property to
label1	All Students:	
listBox1		studentsListBox
button1	Cl&ose	closeeButton
button2	&Print	printButton

Table 8.3 Properties for the DisplayForm controls

Figure 8.14 DisplayForm with all controls

Next, back in the MainForm in the designer window, you will make the "Display" button work.
Double click on the Display button. Inside the button click event handler, add the two lines of code
from below:

```
DisplayForm displayForm = new DisplayForm();
displayForm.ShowDialog();
```

Now, go to the DisplayForm designer window. Double click anywhere on the form, but not on any
controls. This will create the "form load event handler". Any statements written inside this event
handler will be executed when the form loads. Type the following statements inside the "form load
event handler":

```
if (File.Exists("student.txt"))
{
   using StreamReader sr = new StreamReader("student.txt");
   string studentId;
   while ((studentId = sr.ReadLine()) != null)
   {
      string name = sr.ReadLine();
      int score = int.Parse(sr.ReadLine());
      // create a student object
      Student student = new Student(studentId, name, score);
      // add the student to the listbox
      string str = $"Student ID: {student.StudentId}" +
         $" Name: {student.Name}" +
```

```
            $" Grade: {student.GetLetterGrade()}";
         studentsListBox.Items.Add(str);
      }
   }
   else
   {
      MessageBox.Show("Missing student.txt file.");
   }
```

Explanation:

The StreamReader class is very similar to the StreamWriter you used earlier in this chapter. This time you use StreamReader to retrieve data from the student.txt file.

A "while" loop is used to read three lines of text from the student.txt file in each loop; sr.ReadLine() appears three times in the loop, one for reading one line.

A string variable str is assembled before adding it to the listbox.

Next, you will make the "Close" button on the DisplayForm work. Double click on the "Close" button on the DisplayForm in the designer window. Add one line of code Close(); inside the "close button click event handler".

This completes user story 2. Save and run the application.

Test Your Understanding 8.18
The built-in _____ class is used to retrieve data from a text file.
A. Stream
B. StreamWriter
C. StreamReader
D. StreamRetriever

Test Your Understanding 8.19
Suppose you have a listbox control called allStudentListBox on a form. Which of the following statements will add "Hello" to the listbox?
A. allStudentListBox("Hello");
B. allStudentListBox.Add("Hello");
C. allStudentListBox.Items.Add("Hello");
D. allStudentListBox.Items.Last.Add("Hello");

8.8 User Story 3

User Story 3:

As a staff member, I want to be able to search a particular student by student ID so that I can decide if the student is qualified for registration.

Acceptance Criteria: Graphical user interface. When the student ID is entered, only that student's name and letter grade is shown. Letter grade formula is the same as in story 2. The Tiny College requires all students to have a grade of C or higher to qualify for registration.

In this section, you will add a search feature to the application.

Go to the "Solution Explorer" window. Right click on the project. Add a new Windows Form. Name it SearchForm.cs

Back in the MainForm in the designer window, double click on the "Search" button. Add the following code in bold inside the "search button click event handler".

```
SearchForm searchForm = new SearchForm();
searchForm.ShowDialog();
```

Next, go to SearchForm in the design view window. Add the necessary controls so that it looks like Figure 8.15.

Figure 8.15 SearchForm with necessary controls

Then you set the properties of the controls by following the values in Table 8.4:

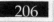

Click once to select	Change "Text" property to	Change "Name" property to
textBox1		searchTextBox
Button1	&Search	searchButton
Button2	Cl&ose	closeButton
Button3	&Print	printButton
groupBox1	Student Found	
label1	Enter Student ID:	
label2	Student ID:	
label3		idLabel
label4	Student Name:	
label5		nameLabel
label6	Letter Grade:	
label7		gradeLebel

Table 8.4 Properties for the controls on the SearchForm

Change the properties of label3, label5, and label7 so that they look like the ones in Figure 8.16 by following the following instructions for Label3:

Click once on Label3 to select it. Set its "AutoSize" property from "true" to "false". This will make it the same size regardless of the text in it. Next, set its "BorderStyle" property from "none" to "Fixed 3D".

Do the same for label5 and label7.

The completed Search form should look like Figure 8.16.

Figure 8.16 The SearchForm with all controls

Analysis:

When this search form loads, you want all data retrieved from the student.txt file to store in a List. When the user types in a student ID and clicks on the "Search" button, the List will be searched. If a match is found, the student data will be displayed in the corresponding labels (the right three labels in Figure 8.16).

Solution:

With SearchForm in the design view window, double click anywhere in the form, but not on any controls. This will create the "form load event handler". Add the following code inside the form load event handler.

```
if (File.Exists("student.txt"))
{
  using StreamReader sr = new StreamReader("student.txt");
  string studentId;
  while ((studentId = sr.ReadLine()) != null)
  {
    string name = sr.ReadLine();
    int score = int.Parse(sr.ReadLine());
    // create a student object
    Student s = new Student(studentId, name, score);
```

```
        // add to the List
        students.Add(s);
    }
}
else
{
    MessageBox.Show("Missing student.txt file.");
}
```

You will notice several red squiggle underscores. You need to insert a line of code to remove the red squiggle. This line (a field) should appear anywhere inside the SearchForm class but outside of any method. You can add it right after the beginning brace of the class {.

```
        List<Student> students = new List<Student>();
```

With all student's data in a List, make the search button work next.

Back with SearchForm in the designer window, double click on the "Search" button. Add the following code inside the "search button click event handler".

```
if (students.Count > 0 &&
    !string.IsNullOrWhiteSpace(searchTextBox.Text))
{
    // search the list, find the student by id
    Student student = students.Find
        (s => s.StudentId == searchTextBox.Text);
    if (student != null)
    {
        idLabel.Text = student.StudentId;
        nameLabel.Text = student.Name;
        gradeLabel.Text = student.GetLetterGrade().ToString();
        printButton.Enabled = true;
    }
    else
    {
        MessageBox.Show("No students found.");
        idLabel.Text = string.Empty;
        nameLabel.Text = string.Empty;
        gradeLabel.Text = string.Empty;
        printButton.Enabled = false;
    }
}
```

```
else
{
    MessageBox.Show("No students or Missing search sring.");
    printButton.Enabled = false;
}
```

Explanation:

The following lines:

```
Student student = students.Find
    (s => s.StudentId == searchTextBox.Text);
```

The operator => is called the Lambda operator. A Lambda expression is a short hand way to write a method. On the left side of the Lambda operator is the input parameter of a method. On the right side are the lambda body statements which correspond to the method body. The lambda statement is to compare a student's StudentId with the search text entered by the user. The whole line will find the first student and store it in a Student object student. The line is similar to the following statements (the question mark ? indicates a nullable type):

```
Student? student = null;
foreach (Student s in students)
{
    if (s.StudentId == searchTextBox.Text)
    {
        student = s;
        break;
    }
}
```

Back with the SearchForm in the design view window, double click on the "Close" button to create the "button click event handler", and add one line of statement inside, Close();

Save and run the application. You should be able to search for a student by student ID.

Test Your Understanding 8.20
A List class in C# has a _____ method you can use to search for an element in the List.
A. Search()
B. Find()
C. SearchFor()
D. FindFor()

Test Your Understanding 8.21
A _____ is a shorthand way of writing a method.

A. Lambda expression
B. Shorthand method
C. Brief method
D. Concise method

Test Your Understanding 8.22
The symbol => is a Lambda operator, the left side of the operator corresponding to the _____ of a method.
A. access modifier
B. return type
C. method name
D. parameter list

8.9 User Story 4

User Story 4:

As a user of the application, I want to be able to print the student record from the application so that I can give it to the students or use it for the convenience of discussion with students.

Acceptance Criteria:

User Story 4: Graphical user interface. The administrator wants to print all records on one document with appropriate headers and date time of printing. The staff wants to print just one student record.

In this section, you will add the print feature to the DisplayForm and SearchForm. First, the DisplayForm:

With the DisplayForm in the design view window, go to the Toolbox, find "printDocument" control, and double click on it to add it to the form's component tray. By default, it will be called printDocument1.

Back to the Display Form in designer view. Double click on the "Print" button. Add one line of code inside the "print button click event handler" as shown below:

```
printDocument1.Print();
```

The above statement calls the Print() method of printDocument1 control. Back in the designer window of the DisplayForm, double click on the "printDocument1" in the component tray. Inside its event handler, add the code below:

```
// print a header
e.Graphics.DrawString("Grade Report",
    new Font("Courier New", 24, FontStyle.Bold),
    Brushes.Black, 300, 100);
// print date and time
e.Graphics.DrawString(DateTime.Now.ToString(),
    new Font("Courier New", 12, FontStyle.Italic),
    Brushes.Black, 320, 150);
// print each student in a loop
int x = 100, y= 200;
foreach(var row in studentsListBox.Items)
{
    e.Graphics.DrawString(row.ToString(),
        new Font("Courier New", 12, FontStyle.Regular),
        Brushes.Black, x, y);
    y += 16;
}
```

Explanation:

In the following line:

Brushes.Black, 300, 100

The first number, 300, indicates the print starts horizontally 300 pixels from the left border of the paper. The second number, 100 indicates, the print starts vertically 100 pixels from the top of the paper. Refer to Figure 8.17 for an example.

The following line:

```
y += 16
```

Adds 16 pixels to the vertical distance when printing the next student. This ensures the next line will be further down.

On paper, it will look like the one on Figure 8.17.

Grade Report

12/24/2021 3:59:13 PM

```
Student ID: 12345 Name: Lynn Smith Grade: C
Student ID: 12346 Name: Lauren Smith Grade: B
```

Figure 8.17 Explanation of print positions in DrawString() method.

The "var" data type in the foreach loop lets the compiler decide the actual data type.

Save and run the application. You should be able to print all the students in the display.

There is one more task for User Story 4. Make the SearchForm print button work.

Have the SearchForm open in the design view window. Go to the Toolbox. Double click on printDocument control to add a printDocument object to the component tray. Use the default name printDocument1.

Double click the Print button on the searchForm and add a single line of code inside the handler.

```
printDocument1.Print();
```

Back in the SearchForm design view window, double click on the printDocument1 in the component tray to create the printPage event handler, and add the following code:

```
e.Graphics.DrawString("Student ID: " + idLabel.Text,
    new Font("Courier New", 12, FontStyle.Regular),
    Brushes.Black, 100, 200);
e.Graphics.DrawString("Student Name: " + nameLabel.Text,
    new Font("Courier New", 12, FontStyle.Regular),
    Brushes.Black, 100, 220);
e.Graphics.DrawString("Student Grade: " + gradeLabel.Text,
    new Font("Courier New", 12, FontStyle.Regular),
    Brushes.Black, 100, 240);
```

Save and run the program to test all features.

Test Your Understanding 8.23
There are two steps to making a print button on a form work. What are these two steps?

A. the print button click event calls the printDocument's print() method, which will trigger the printDocument's printPage event.
B. the print button click event calls the button's print() method, which will trigger the printDocument's printPage event.
C. the print button click event calls the printDocument's printPage() method, which will trigger the printDocument's printPage event.
D. the print button click event calls the printPage's print() method, which will trigger the printDocument's printPage event.

Test Your Understanding 8.24
Which of the following statements about print is correct?
1) The statement printDocument1.Print(); will print everything on the form.
2) The text you want to print should be included inside the printDocument's printPage event handler.
A. 1) only
B. 2) only
C. Both 1) and 2)
D. Neither 1) nor 2)

Programming Challenge 8.1
Create an application that allows the user to enter an employee's payroll information. It allows the user to enter a new employee, add hours worked, and display all employee information. A sample MainForm is shown in Figure 8.18.

Figure 8.18 Sample MainForm.

The "Add Employee" form is shown in Figure 8.19.

Figure 8.19 Add Employee Form

The save button on the form will save the new employee into a text file employee.txt in the default folder. The "Add Hours" form is shown in Figure 8.20.

Figure 8.20 Form for entering an employee's hours worked.

In the form, the first employee from employee.txt should be displayed. Then, the user enters hours worked and clicks on the next button. The hours worked should be added to a List of employees, and the second employee data is displayed and expects the user to enter hours worked. When all hours worked data are entered, a pop up will display "no more employees". The user can then click on "Close & Save", which will close the form and save all data to the same employee.txt file.

The "Display All" form is shown in Figure 8.21:

Figure 8.21 Form for displaying all employees.

The "Print" button in Figure 8.21 will print all employee data in a nicely formatted way on paper. The "Exit" button on the MainForm will exit the program. A class called Employee must be used for all three features (Add Employee, Add Hours, and Display All).

8.10 Agile Summary

You have learned the roles, events, and artifacts of agile in the previous chapters. It's time for a summary.

Your agile team starts with the software requirements from the business. Start writing user stories based on the requirements and put the stories in the product backlog. Some stories can be easily written while others may be vague and need clarification from the business. The stories are estimated by the team members for the effort needed to implement each story. Product owner is in charge of the product backlog and the product backlog is updated frequently. Stories in the product backlog are prioritized with different granularity.

Your team will move a certain number of stories from the product backlog to the sprint backlog based on the team velocity. In the sprint planning, the team will break each story into smaller and more manageable tasks. Each task is then estimated by the amount of time needed to complete it.

On a daily basis, the team holds a brief daily scrum meeting to see what each member has done yesterday, plans to do today, and any impediments encountered. Progress may be recorded on the Kanban board and/or burn down chart.

At the end of the sprint, after the new piece of software is integrated into the existing software, the team will hold an informal sprint review to demo the increment to the customers. Next, the team will hold a sprint retrospective meeting to examine how the team can do better in the next sprint.

This brings us back to another sprint until the project is completed.

Test Your Understanding 8.25
Which of the following is the first meeting of a sprint?
A. Sprint planning
B. Daily scrum
C. Sprint review
D. Retrospective

Test Your Understanding 8.26
Which of the following is the last meeting of a sprint?
A. Sprint planning
B. Daily scrum
C. Sprint review
D. Retrospective

8.11 Chapter Summary

In this chapter, you learned how to create a windows forms application, how to write and read from an external text file, how to search a List to find a matching element, how to display a group of elements in a ListBox, and how to print content from a form.

You also learned how to break up a project into sprints and complete one sprint at a time. User requirements are expressed in the form of user stories. Each sprint completes one or more user stories.

8.12 Solution to Programming Challenge

Programming Challenge 8.1 (You must follow the same steps in the Example 8.1. If you just type the code from this section for each form, it will not work. Also, we on purposely omit the code for close form, you should still add it.)

Code for Employee.cs

```csharp
internal class Employee
{
    // fields
    private string employeeId;
    private string name;
    private decimal payRate;
    private decimal hoursWorked;
    // constructors
    public Employee(string employeeId, string name,
        decimal payRate)
    {
        this.employeeId = employeeId;
        this.name – name;
        this.payRate = payRate;
    }
    public Employee(string employeeId, string name,
        decimal payRate, decimal hoursWorked)
    {
        this.employeeId = employeeId;
        this.name = name;
        this.payRate = payRate;
        this.hoursWorked = hoursWorked;
    }
    // properties
    public string EmployeeId
    {
        get { return employeeId; }
        set { employeeId = value; }
    }
    public string Name
    {
        get { return name; }
        set { name = value; }
    }
    public decimal PayRate
    {
```

```
      get { return payRate; }
      set { payRate = value; }
    }
    public decimal HoursWorked
    {
      get { return hoursWorked; }
      set { hoursWorked = value; }
    }
    // method
    public decimal PayAmount()
    {
      decimal amount;
      amount = PayRate * HoursWorked;
      return amount;
    }
    // ToString
    public override string ToString()
    {
      string str;
      str = $"{EmployeeId}\n{Name}\n{PayRate}\n{HoursWorked}";
      return str;
    }
  }
```

Code for the MainForm

```
public partial class MainForm : Form
{
  public MainForm()
  {
    InitializeComponent();
  }
  private void addEmployeeButton_Click(object sender, EventArgs e)
  {
    AddEmployeeForm addEmployeeForm = new AddEmployeeForm();
    addEmployeeForm.ShowDialog();
  }
  private void addHoursWorkedButton_Click(object sender, EventArgs e)
  {
    AddHoursForm addHoursForm = new AddHoursForm();
    addHoursForm.ShowDialog();
  }
  private void displayAllButton_Click(object sender, EventArgs e)
  {
```

```csharp
    DisplayAllForm displayAllForm = new DisplayAllForm();
    displayAllForm.ShowDialog();
  }
}
```

Code for the Add Employee Form:

```csharp
public partial class AddEmployeeForm : Form
{
    public AddEmployeeForm()
    {
        InitializeComponent();
    }
    private void saveButton_Click(object sender, EventArgs e)
    {
        using StreamWriter sw = File.AppendText("employee.txt");
        if (!(string.IsNullOrWhiteSpace(idTextBox.Text) ||
            string.IsNullOrWhiteSpace(nameTextBox.Text) ||
            string.IsNullOrWhiteSpace(payRateTextBox.Text)))
        {
            if (decimal.TryParse(payRateTextBox.Text,
                        out decimal payRate)
            && payRate >= 0)
            {
                // make an object from the data entry form
                Employee employee = new Employee
                    (idTextBox.Text, nameTextBox.Text, payRate);
                // save the employee record to the file
                sw.WriteLine(employee);
                // clear the textboxes
                clearButton.PerformClick();
            }
            else
            {
                MessageBox.Show("Pay rate must be a number.");
            }
        }
        else
        {
            MessageBox.Show("All fields are required.");
        }
    }
    private void clearButton_Click(object sender, EventArgs e)
    {
        idTextBox.Clear();
```

```
        nameTextBox.Clear();
        payRateTextBox.Clear();
        idTextBox.Focus();
    }
}
```

Code for Add Hours Form

```csharp
public partial class AddHoursForm : Form
{
    List<Employee> employees = new List<Employee>();
    public AddHoursForm()
    {
        InitializeComponent();
    }

    private void AddHoursForm_Load(object sender, EventArgs e)
    {
        // remove the controlBox on top right
        ControlBox = false;
        if (File.Exists("employee.txt"))
        {
            using StreamReader sr =
                new StreamReader("employee.txt");
            string employeeId;
            while ((employeeId = sr.ReadLine()) != null)
            {
                Employee employee = new Employee(employeeId,
                    sr.ReadLine(),
                    decimal.Parse(sr.ReadLine()),
                    decimal.Parse(sr.ReadLine()));
                employees.Add(employee);
            }
            // display first employee
            if (employees.Count > 0)
            {
                idLabel.Text = employees[0].EmployeeId;
                nameLabel.Text = employees[0].Name;
            }
            else
            {
                MessageBox.Show("No employees in the file.");
                nextButton.Enabled = false;
            }
        }
        else
```

```csharp
        {
            MessageBox.Show("Missing employee.txt");
            nextButton.Enabled = false;
        }


    }
    int count = 1; // this is a field
    private void nextButton_Click(object sender, EventArgs e)
    {
        if (decimal.TryParse(hoursTextBox.Text,
            out decimal hours)
            && hours >= 0)
        {
            // add hours worked to the array
            employees[count - 1].HoursWorked = hours;
            if (count < employees.Count)
            {
                idLabel.Text = employees[count].EmployeeId;
                nameLabel.Text = employees[count].Name;
                count++;
            }
            else
            {
                MessageBox.Show("no more records.");
                nextButton.Enabled = false;
            }
        }
        else
        {
            MessageBox.Show("Hours worked must be a number.");
        }
        clearButton.PerformClick();
    }

private void closeAndSaveButton_Click(object sender, EventArgs e)
    {
        using StreamWriter sw = File.CreateText("employee.txt");
        foreach (Employee employee in employees)
        {
            sw.WriteLine(employee);
        }
        Close();
    }
    private void clearButton_Click(object sender, EventArgs e)
    {
        hoursTextBox.Clear();
```

```csharp
        hoursTextBox.Focus();
    }
}
```

Code for Display all employees Form:

```csharp
public partial class DisplayAllForm : Form
{
    public DisplayAllForm()
    {
        InitializeComponent();
    }

    private void DisplayAllForm_Load(object sender, EventArgs e)
    {
        if (File.Exists("employee.txt"))
        {
            using StreamReader sr =
                new StreamReader("employee.txt");
            string employeeId;
            while ((employeeId = sr.ReadLine()) != null)
            {
                string name = sr.ReadLine();
                decimal payRate = decimal.Parse(sr.ReadLine());
                decimal hoursWorked =
                    decimal.Parse(sr.ReadLine());
                // create an employee object
                Employee employee = new Employee(employeeId,
                    name, payRate, hoursWorked);
                // add the employee to the listbox
            string str = $"Employee ID: {employee.EmployeeId}" +
                    $" Name: {employee.Name}" +
                    $" Pay Amount: {employee.PayAmount():C}";
                employeesListBox.Items.Add(str);
            }
        }
        else
        {
            MessageBox.Show("Missing employee.txt file.");
        }
    }

    private void printButton_Click(object sender, EventArgs e)
    {
        printDocument1.Print();
```

```csharp
    }

    private void printDocument1_PrintPage(object sender,
        System.Drawing.Printing.PrintPageEventArgs e)
    {
        // print a header
        e.Graphics.DrawString("Employee Payroll",
            new Font("Courier New", 24, FontStyle.Bold),
            Brushes.Black, 250, 100);
        // print date and time
        e.Graphics.DrawString(DateTime.Now.ToString(),
            new Font("Courier New", 12, FontStyle.Italic),
            Brushes.Black, 300, 150);
        // print each employee in a loop
        int x = 100, y = 200;
        foreach (var row in employeesListBox.Items)
        {
            e.Graphics.DrawString(row.ToString(),
                new Font("Courier New", 12, FontStyle.Regular),
                Brushes.Black, x, y);
            y += 16;
        }
    }
}
```

8.13 Solutions to Test Your Understanding

8.1 A; 8.2 C; 8.3 D; 8.4 C; 8.5 D; 8.6 D; 8.7 D; 8.8 C; 8.9 A; 8.10 C; 8.11 B; 8.12 B; 8.13 C; 8.14 B; 8.15 C; 8.16 D; 8.17 C; 8.18 C; 8.19 C; 8.20 B; 8.21 A; 8.22 D; 8.23 A; 8.24 B; 8.25 A; 8.26 D;

Chapter 9: Case Study

9.1 Develop simple C# Windows Form application by following agile principles.

9.1 Case Background

In this chapter, you will be working on an agile team to develop an inventory management system for Mr. Lincoln (introduced in Chapter 1). Find two or three classmates or friends who are interested in agile software development to work together on this case study.

Dragon Phoenix Toy (DPT) LLC is a tiny retailer founded in 1994. It sells about 50 types of toys and most of them are seasonal. The manager wants a simple desktop application that can handle the company's inventory.

A product in DPT has a product ID, product name, product description, sales price, and inventory on hand.

When a shipment of new products arrives, the manager wants to be able to enter the product information into the system.

When a shipment of existing products arrives, the manager wants to be able to update the inventory on hand.

When a purchase is made by a customer, the check-out associate wants to enter the product ID and units sold. One sale can include multiple products. When all sale items are entered, the form should display a receipt which includes the name of each product sold, units sold, line total, subtotal, tax (9%), and total charge. The manager wants the inventory on hand to be updated after each sale. The application should be able to display and print the receipt similar to the following format.

```
Dragon Phoenix Toy (DPT)
        123 Toys St.
     Argentina OK 48451
   11/12/2022 2:30:03 PM
Wooden Train      2         40.00
Doll              1         30.00
Sub total                   70.00
Tax                          6.30
Total                       76.30
```

From time to time, the manager wants to check the product inventory and print it out. The print sheet should include the date and time of when the inventory was checked

All data should be saved in a text file in its default location.

9.2 Your Tasks

Your tasks as a team:

1. Build the Product Backlog:

    1a. Write the user stories.

    1b. Prioritize the stories.

    1c. Estimate the story points for each story.

2. Build the Sprint Backlog:

    2a. Write sprint goals.

2b. Pick stories from the product backlog.

2c. Strategy to reach the goals.

3. Start a sprint planning:

3a. Break each story down to its component tasks if necessary.

3b. Estimate hours of work needed for each task.

4. Each member picks a task to work for a day or less. Use paired programming if possible.

5. Have daily stand-up meetings, and after the meeting, each member picks tasks to work on.

6. At the end of the sprint, conduct a sprint review/demo the deliverable to the customer.

7. Retrospection. As a team, find out what works and what doesn't. How can you do better in the next sprint?

8. Repeat steps 2 to 7 above for another sprint.

Find a few people to work with before checking the solution.

9.3 User Stories.

1. Possible user stories

User Story 1: As the owner, I want to check the inventory at any time so that I know how the business runs.

Acceptance Criterion: Graphical user interface. With a click of a button, the current inventory is displayed. Use a red color on print to indicate a low inventory item (less than 3 units in stock).

User Story 2: As the owner, I want to update the inventory when a new shipment arrives so that I have up to date inventory.

Acceptance Criterion: User enters the product ID (simulating bar code scan) and the new shipment quantity, click on "Update" to update the inventory.

User Story 3: As the owner, I want to enter new product information into the system before a new shipment arrives.

Acceptance Criterion: User can enter new product information without the quantity. The quantity can be updated later.

User Story 4: As a cashier, I want to enter order information and the inventory is automatically updated so that I don't need to keep the record on paper.

Acceptance Criterion: An order can contain multiple product items with varying quantity. Inventory should be updated as the order is submitted.

User Story 5: As a cashier, I want to print the receipt for an order for the customer so that the customer has the proof of purchase.

Acceptance Criterion: The receipt should be similar to the one displayed in the problem description earlier in this chapter. The order details should be displayed before printing. The receipt data are not saved in a text file.

User Story 6: As the owner, I want to print my inventory on paper so that I can take it anywhere I want.

Acceptance Criterion: The inventory print is on the regular print paper and looks professional with the date and time on it. Display the details before printing.

9.4 Prioritize the Stories

The product owner decides that the priority of the stories should be as follows with the first one as the most important:

Story 3, Story 2, Story 1, Story 4, Story 5, Story 6.

9.5 Estimate the Story Points for each Story

The team plays the Poker Planning Game. If you don't remember the game, you can go back and read it again (in Chapter 5). At first, the members don't know what each number exactly means and are not comfortable with which number to place. All of them know that ½ is the easiest story and 100 is the most difficult one. After a few rounds of play, they decide 8 story points as the estimate for story 1.

The estimate for the next story is easier. If a member thinks story 2 is more difficult than story 1, he or she will place a number larger than 8. Otherwise, a smaller number is placed. After a few rounds of play, they decide story 2 is 40 points.

One benefit of estimating story points is getting to know more about each story. Some stories may be more difficult than they look. For example, Story 2 was first estimated by the members as 5, 5, 5, and 100. Even though the majority estimate it for 5 points, the member who gave 100 points explains that the difficulty is due to the fact that an update on a text file is not as easy as an update on a database. It is not difficult to read the specific inventory on hand from the file. Also, it is not difficult to update that number once it is in the program. However, it is difficult to save it back to the original location in the text file. One member suggests that maybe they should retrieve all data instead of just one inventory on hand. This way, after updating, the whole list of data can be saved back to the file without worrying about the original location, since the old one will be completely erased and replaced with the new inventories. Now, they believe they understand the problem better and in the second play, they give the estimate as 40.

The team continues to play and estimates 5 points for Story 3. They believe saving data to a text file is not much different from reading it from the file, as they already learned in Chapter 8.

They estimate 40 points for Story 4. They don't know how to handle an order with multiple items.

They estimate 8 points for Story 5 because they learned how to print from Chapter 8. The only challenge is how to display the date and time.

Finally, they estimate 5 points for Story 6. They believe with the experience from Story 5, they can handle it in less time for the print feature.

9.6 Sprint One (Zero)

The team members have a full-time job somewhere and cannot work on this in a full-time manner. Each member says he or she can devote about 5 hours per week to the project. They don't want a long sprint. They decide to have a time-box of two weeks for each sprint so that they can get feedback sooner. The total story points are 106 (8+40+5+40+8+5). They pick stories one, two, and three for the first sprint with a team velocity of 53 points.

9.6.1 Sprint Planning

The team identified the tasks for Story 3:

Story 3 Tasks (3 hours):

Main Form (Figure 9.1) and Story 3 user interface (Figure 9.2) (1 hours).

Product class (1 hours).

Save data to the text file (1 hour).

Tasks for Story 2 (10 hours):

Story 2 user interface (Figure 9.3) (1 hours).

Read the inventory from the text file (2 hours).

Update the inventory (5 hours).

Save the updated inventory back to the text file (2 hours).

Story 1 user interface (Figure 9.4) (2 hours).

Read data from the text file, and display on the form (Figure 9.4) (2 hours).

9.6.2 Working on the project

They decide to use pair programming. Since they cannot physically meet, they decide to use remote PC access to work on one screen with two members. Each pair picks some tasks to work on.

9.6.3 Sprint Review

At the end of the sprint, they put all applications together and demo it to a friend pretending to be Mr. Lincoln, the store owner, and see how close they meet the requirements.

9.6.4 Retrospective

As a team, they hold a video conference meeting and discuss what works and what does not work, and what new techniques they want to try in the next sprint.

9.7 Sprint Two

In the second sprint, the team works on the remaining stories by following the same pattern as sprint one.

9.8 Release

By the end of the four weeks, they believe they have achieved what Mr. Lincoln wants and deploy the software on Mr. Lincoln's computer.

9.9 Product Class and Order Class

There are two custom classes you will need for this application: a Product class and an Order class. Create a product class which includes product ID, name, description, price, inventory on hand, units sold, and whether it is the correct order.

```csharp
namespace Chapter9Example1
{
    internal class Product
    {
        // fields
        private string productId;
        private string name;
        private string description;
        private decimal price;
        private int onHand;
        private int unitSold;
        private bool isInOrder;
        // properties
        public string ProductId
        {
            get { return productId; }
            set { productId = value; }
        }
        public string Name
        {
            get { return name; }
            set { name = value; }
        }
        public string Description
        {
            get { return description; }
            set { description = value; }
        }
    }
```

```csharp
    public decimal Price
    {
        get { return price; }
        set { price = value; }
    }
    public int OnHand
    {
        get { return onHand; }
        set { onHand = value; }
    }
    public int UnitSold
    {
        get { return unitSold; }
        set { unitSold = value; }
    }
    public bool IsInOrder
    {
        get { return isInOrder; }
        set { isInOrder = value; }
    }
    // constructors
    public Product(string productId, string name, string description,
        decimal price, int onHand)
    {
        this.productId = productId;
        this.name = name;
        this.description = description;
        this.price = price;
        this.onHand = onHand;

    }
    public Product(string productId, int unitSold)
    {
        this.productId = productId;
        this.unitSold = unitSold;
    }

    // methods
    public decimal CalculateProductCost()
    {
        decimal cost;
        cost = Price * UnitSold;
        return cost;
    }
    public void Sold()
    {
        OnHand -= UnitSold;
    }
    // ToString
    public override string ToString()
    {
        string str;
        str = $"{productId}\n{Name}\n{Description}\n{Price}\n{OnHand}";
        return str;
    }
  }
}
```

Next, create an order class that includes a List of products, their corresponding quantities ordered, and calculation of subtotal, tax, and total.

```csharp
namespace Chapter9Example1
{
    internal class Order
    {
        // fields
        public const decimal TAX_RATE = 0.09M;
        private List<Product> productInOrder;
        // property
        public List<Product> ProductInOrder
        {
            get { return productInOrder; }
            set { productInOrder = value; }
        }
        // constructor
        public Order(List<Product> productInOrder)
        {

            this.productInOrder = productInOrder;
        }
        // methods
        public decimal CalculateSubTotal()
        {
            decimal subTotal = 0;
            foreach (Product p in productInOrder)
            {
                subTotal += p.CalculateProductCost();
            }
            return subTotal;
        }
        public decimal CalculateTax()
        {
            decimal taxAmount;
            taxAmount = CalculateSubTotal() * TAX_RATE;
            return taxAmount;
        }
        public decimal CalculateTotal()
        {
            decimal total;
            total = CalculateSubTotal() + CalculateTax();
            return total;
        }
        //ToString
        public override string ToString()
        {
            string str;
            str = $"   Dragon Phoenix Toy\n";
            str += $"     123 Toy St.\n";
            str += $"   Argentina OK 48451\n";
            str += $"   " + DateTime.Now.ToString() +"\n";
        foreach (Product p in productInOrder)
        {
            str += $"{p.Name, -15}{p.UnitSold, -2}{p.CalculateProductCost(), 10:n2}\n";
```

```
        }
        str += $"{"Sub total:", 15}{CalculateSubTotal(), 10:n2}\n";
        str += $"{"Tax:", 15}{CalculateTax(), 10:n2}\n";
        str += $"{"Total:",15}{CalculateTotal(),10:n2}";
        return str;
        }
    }
}
```

9.10 The Main Form

A MainForm with buttons that will open up new forms for each feature.

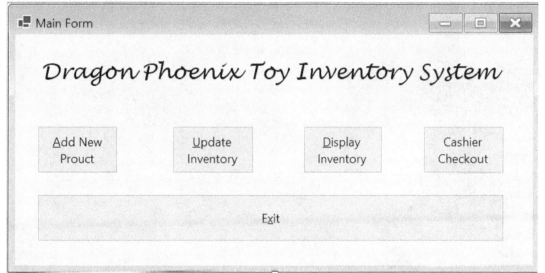

Figure 9.1 The MainForm and its controls

Code for the MainForm omitted for brevity.

9.11 The Add New Product Form

When the "Add New Product" button is clicked, this form will open.

An AddNewProductForm that allows the user to enter new product information.

Figure 9.2 Add New Product Form
Code for AddNewProductForm.

```csharp
namespace Chapter9Example1
{
  public partial class AddNewProductForm : Form
  {
    List<Product> products = new List<Product>();
    public AddNewProductForm()
    {
      InitializeComponent();
    }
    private void clearButton_Click(object sender, EventArgs e)
    {
      idTextBox.Clear();
      nameTextBox.Clear();
      descriptionTextBox.Clear();
      priceTextBox.Clear();
      quantityTextBox.Clear();
      idTextBox.Focus();
    }
    private void AddNewProductForm_Load(object sender, EventArgs e)
    {
      if (File.Exists("product.txt"))
      {
        using StreamReader sr = new StreamReader("product.txt");
        string id;
        while ((id = sr.ReadLine()) != null)
        {
          Product p = new Product(id, sr.ReadLine(), sr.ReadLine(),
            decimal.Parse(sr.ReadLine()), int.Parse(sr.ReadLine()));
          products.Add(p);
        }
      }
      else
      {
```

```csharp
            MessageBox.Show("Missing product.txt file.");
        }
    }
    private void saveButton_Click(object sender, EventArgs e)
    {
        using StreamWriter sw = File.AppendText("product.txt");
        decimal price;
        int onHand = 0;
        if (string.IsNullOrEmpty(idTextBox.Text) ||
            (products.Find(x => x.ProductId == idTextBox.Text) != null))
        {
            MessageBox.Show("ID is already used.");
            idTextBox.Focus();
            idTextBox.SelectAll();
        }
        else if (string.IsNullOrEmpty(nameTextBox.Text))
        {
            MessageBox.Show("Product name cannot be empty");
            nameTextBox.Focus();
        }
        else if (string.IsNullOrEmpty(descriptionTextBox.Text))
        {
            MessageBox.Show("Description cannot be empty");
            descriptionTextBox.Focus();
        }
        else if (!decimal.TryParse(priceTextBox.Text, out price) ||
            price < 0)
        {
            MessageBox.Show("Price is required and must be a number.");
            priceTextBox.Focus();
            priceTextBox.SelectAll();
        }
        else if (!string.IsNullOrEmpty(quantityTextBox.Text) &&
            !int.TryParse(quantityTextBox.Text, out onHand) ||
            onHand < 0)
        {
            MessageBox.Show("Qunatity must be a number or empty");
            quantityTextBox.Focus();
            quantityTextBox.SelectAll();
        }
        else
        {
            Product product = new Product(idTextBox.Text,
                nameTextBox.Text, descriptionTextBox.Text,
                price, onHand);
            sw.WriteLine(product);
            MessageBox.Show("Record saved.");
            clearButton.PerformClick();
        }
    }
}
}
```

9.12 The Update Product Form

An UpdateProductForm that allows the user to update the inventory on hand by searching the product ID. The user can then enter the quantity in the shipment for that product.

Figure 9.3 Update Product Form (ReadOnly property for on hand textbox is true.)

Code for UpdateProductForm.

```csharp
namespace Chapter9Example1
{
    public partial class UpdateProductForm : Form
    {
        List<Product> products = new List<Product>();
        public UpdateProductForm()
        {
            InitializeComponent();
        }
        private void UpdateProductForm_Load(object sender, EventArgs e)
        {
            if (File.Exists("product.txt"))
            {
                using StreamReader sr = new StreamReader("product.txt");
                string id;
                while ((id = sr.ReadLine()) != null)
                {
                    Product p = new Product(id, sr.ReadLine(), sr.ReadLine(),
                        decimal.Parse(sr.ReadLine()), int.Parse(sr.ReadLine()));
                    products.Add(p);
                }
                updateButton.Enabled = false;
            }
            else
            {
```

```csharp
            MessageBox.Show("Missing product.txt file.");
            Close();
        }


}
private void clearButton_Click(object sender, EventArgs e)
{
    idTextBox.Clear();
    nameTextBox.Clear();
    descriptionTextBox.Clear();
    priceTextBox.Clear();
    quantityTextBox.Clear();
    newQuantityTextBox.Clear();
    idTextBox.ReadOnly = false;
    idTextBox.Focus();
}
private void findButton_Click(object sender, EventArgs e)
{
    Product product = products.Find(p => p.ProductId == idTextBox.Text);
    if (product != null)
    {
        idTextBox.Text = product.ProductId;
        idTextBox.ReadOnly = true;
        nameTextBox.Text = product.Name;
        descriptionTextBox.Text = product.Description;
        priceTextBox.Text = product.Price.ToString();
        quantityTextBox.Text = product.OnHand.ToString();
        updateButton.Enabled = true;
    }
    else
    {
        MessageBox.Show("No product with that ID found.");
        idTextBox.Focus();
        idTextBox.SelectAll();
    }
}
private void updateButton_Click(object sender, EventArgs e)
{
    int index = products.FindIndex(x => x.ProductId == idTextBox.Text);
    using StreamWriter sw = File.AppendText("product.txt");
    decimal price;
    int onHand = 0;
    int newArrival = 0;
    if (string.IsNullOrEmpty(nameTextBox.Text))
    {
        MessageBox.Show("Product name cannot be empty");
        nameTextBox.Focus();
    }
    else if (string.IsNullOrEmpty(descriptionTextBox.Text))
    {
        MessageBox.Show("Description cannot be empty");
        descriptionTextBox.Focus();
    }
    else if (!decimal.TryParse(priceTextBox.Text, out price) ||
        price < 0)
    {
        MessageBox.Show("Price is required and must be a number.");
        priceTextBox.Focus();
```

```csharp
            priceTextBox.SelectAll();
        }
        else if (!string.IsNullOrEmpty(newQuantityTextBox.Text) &&
            !int.TryParse(newQuantityTextBox.Text, out newArrival) ||
            newArrival < 0)
        {
            MessageBox.Show("New qunatity must be a number or empty");
            newQuantityTextBox.Focus();
            newQuantityTextBox.SelectAll();
        }
        else
        {
            products[index].Name = nameTextBox.Text;
            products[index].Description = descriptionTextBox.Text;
            products[index].Price = price;
            products[index].OnHand += newArrival;
            MessageBox.Show("Product updated.");
            clearButton.PerformClick();
            idTextBox.ReadOnly = false;
        }
    }
    private void saveAndCloseButton_Click(object sender, EventArgs e)
    {
        using StreamWriter sr = File.CreateText("product.txt");
        foreach (Product product in products)
        {
            sr.WriteLine(product);
        }
        Close();
    }
}
}
```

9.13 The Display Product Form

A DisplayProductForm that will show all products in the inventory. The form will also allow the user to print the inventory.

Figure 9.4 Display Product Form

Code for DisplayProductForm.

```csharp
namespace Chapter9Example1
{
    public partial class DisplayProductForm : Form
    {
        List<Product> products = new List<Product>();
        public DisplayProductForm()
        {
            InitializeComponent();
        }

        private void DisplayProductForm_Load(object sender, EventArgs e)
        {
            if (File.Exists("product.txt"))
            {
                using StreamReader sr =
                    new StreamReader("product.txt");
                string productId;
                while ((productId = sr.ReadLine()) != null)
                {
                    string name = sr.ReadLine();
                    string description = sr.ReadLine();
                    decimal price = decimal.Parse(sr.ReadLine());
                    int onHand = int.Parse(sr.ReadLine());
                    Product product = new Product(productId,
                        name, description, price, onHand);
                    products.Add(product);
                    string str = $"Product ID: {product.ProductId}" +
                        $" Name: {product.Name}" +
                        $" Description: {product.Description}" +
                        $" Price: {product.Price:C}" +
                        $" On Hand: {product.OnHand}";
                    inventoryListBox.Items.Add(str);
                }
            }
        }
```

```csharp
        else
        {
            MessageBox.Show("Missing product.txt file.");
        }
    }

    private void printButton_Click(object sender, EventArgs e)
    {
        printDocument1.Print();
    }

    private void printDocument1_PrintPage(object sender,
            System.Drawing.Printing.PrintPageEventArgs e)
    {
        e.Graphics.DrawString("Inventory",
            new Font("Courier New", 24, FontStyle.Bold),
            Brushes.Black, 350, 100);
        e.Graphics.DrawString(DateTime.Now.ToString(),
            new Font("Courier New", 12, FontStyle.Italic),
            Brushes.Black, 330, 150);
        int x = 100, y = 200;
        foreach (var product in products)
        {
            e.Graphics.DrawString($"Product ID: {product.ProductId}"+
                $" Product Name: {product.Name}",
                new Font("Courier New", 12, FontStyle.Regular),
                Brushes.Black, x, y);
            y += 16;
            e.Graphics.DrawString($"Description: {product.Description}",
                new Font("Courier New", 12, FontStyle.Regular),
                Brushes.Black, x, y);
            y += 16;
            e.Graphics.DrawString($"Price: {product.Price}" +
                $" Quantity: {product.OnHand}",
                new Font("Courier New", 12, FontStyle.Regular),
                product.OnHand<3? Brushes.Red:Brushes.Black, x, y);
            y += 16;
            e.Graphics.DrawString($"",
                new Font("Courier New", 12, FontStyle.Regular),
                Brushes.Black, x, y);
            y += 16;
        }
    }
}
```

9.14 The Check Out Form

A CheckOutForm that allows the cashier to enter each product ID and item quantity of an order. On this form, an order should be printed when all purchased items are entered.

Figure 9.5 CheckOut Form

Code for CheckOutForm.

```csharp
using System.Data;

namespace Chapter9Example1
{
    public partial class CheckoutForm : Form
    {
        public CheckoutForm()
        {
            InitializeComponent();
        }
        Order order;
        List<Product> products = new List<Product>();
        List<Product> productsInOrder = new List<Product>();
        private void CheckoutForm_Load(object sender, EventArgs e)
        {
            if (File.Exists("product.txt"))
            {
                using StreamReader sr =
                    new StreamReader("product.txt");
                string productId;
                while ((productId = sr.ReadLine()) != null)
                {
                    string name = sr.ReadLine();
                    string description = sr.ReadLine();
                    decimal price = decimal.Parse(sr.ReadLine());
                    int onHand = int.Parse(sr.ReadLine());
                    Product product = new Product(productId,
                        name, description, price, onHand);
                    products.Add(product);
```

```csharp
        }
    }
}

private void addToOrderButton_Click(object sender, EventArgs e)
{
    int unitSold =0;
    if (products.Find(x => x.ProductId == idTextBox.Text) == null)
    {
        MessageBox.Show("ID does not exists.");
        idTextBox.Focus();
        idTextBox.SelectAll();
    }
    else if (string.IsNullOrEmpty(unitsTextBox.Text) ||
        !int.TryParse(unitsTextBox.Text, out unitSold) ||
        unitSold < 1)
    {
        MessageBox.Show("Unit Sold must be a whole number");
        unitsTextBox.Focus();
        unitsTextBox.SelectAll();
    }
    else
    {
        int index = products.FindIndex(p => p.ProductId == idTextBox.Text);
        if (products[index].OnHand >= unitSold)
        {
            products[index].UnitSold += unitSold;
            products[index].OnHand -= unitSold;
            products[index].IsInOrder = true;
            orderListBox.Font = new Font("Courier New", 12);
            orderListBox.Items.Add($"{products[index].Name}" +
                $" {unitSold} {unitSold * products[index].Price:C}");
            idTextBox.Clear();
            idTextBox.Focus();
        }
        else
        {
            MessageBox.Show("Not enough inventory.");
            unitsTextBox.Focus();
            unitsTextBox.SelectAll();
        }
    }

}

private void readyToPayButton_Click(object sender, EventArgs e)
{
    productsInOrder = products.Where(p => p.IsInOrder == true).ToList();
    orderListBox.Items.Clear();
    order = new Order(productsInOrder);
    orderListBox.Items.AddRange(order.ToString().Split('\n'));
    addToOrderButton.Enabled = false;

}

private void printButton_Click(object sender, EventArgs e)
{
    printDocument1.Print();
```

```
        }

    private void printDocument1_PrintPage(object sender,
        System.Drawing.Printing.PrintPageEventArgs e)
    {
      if (order == null)
      {
        MessageBox.Show("Sorry, no orders found.");
      }
      else
      {
        e.Graphics.DrawString(order.ToString(), new Font("Courier New", 12,
          FontStyle.Regular),
          Brushes.Black, 50, 100);
      }

    }

    private void saveAndCloseButton_Click(object sender, EventArgs e)
    {
      using StreamWriter sr = File.CreateText("product.txt");
      foreach (Product product in products)
      {
        sr.WriteLine(product);
      }
      Close();
    }
  }
}
```

9.15 Save and Test the Application

After you type all the code, correct any compiler errors. You should test the application with valid inputs and invalid inputs.

Programming Challenge 9.1

Tiny College is a small college with less than 100 students at any time. It offers a handful of courses in Math and English to help those who want to go back to college, but are not academically ready.

The college needs a simple GUI desktop application that can help them keep track of the course registration. All course registrations must go through the secretary with a paper form filled out by a student. The college already has a student record system that takes care of all student data, so this new system will keep track of who (a student ID) registers what class. The application is just about the courses and corresponding student IDs who registered the course.

The application should include and use a class called Course. A course has a course ID, course title, course description, seating capacity, and a list of student IDs who registered the course. The application should allow the administrators to add new courses, update a course, or remove a course with no students enrolled. It should also allow the administrators to add more seats to a class that is already open for registration. The data about courses should be stored in an external text file.

When the secretary registers a new student, the student ID is added to the course and the available seat should be deducted by 1. When the class is full, no more students can be registered (the administrator can add more seats though). The application should let the administrators display and print all course information and the students enrolled. The application should let the secretary display and print a registration record for a student (the student may register for more than one course at the time).

Your Tasks as a team:
Same as the tasks listed in Section 9.2.

Programming Challenge 9.2

Tiny College is a small college with less than 100 students at any time.
The college needs a simple GUI desktop application that can allow an instructor to create, update, or delete a quiz question through the application. The instructor can pick a file name for each quiz. It also allows students to pick a quiz to take.

When a student completes a quiz, there is a summary form displaying the student's correct and incorrect answers. For the incorrect response, it should also show the correct answer. It also shows the student's percentage of correct and total time taken for the quiz.

A quiz is saved in an external text file and contains several quiz questions. Each quiz question contains a question and four possible answers, and ends with the key. For example,

```
Where is the capital of the state of Indiana?
Indianapolis
Fort Wayne
Bloomington
Terre Haute
Indianapolis
```

The last line is the correct answer. It must be one of the four options.

Your Tasks as a team:

Same as the tasks listed in Section 9.2

Programming Challenge 9.3

The Tiny Library needs an application to keep track of its books.

A book has a title, author name(s) (all in one string separated by a semicolon ;), original number of copies, and available copies.

A librarian should be able to add a new book into the library and update its original number of copies when a new copy of an existing book is purchased, or a copy is reported missing.

When a book is checked out, the number of available copies of that book is deducted by one. One cannot check out a book if its available copies are zero. When a book is returned, the number of available copies is increased by one.

The library does not keep track of its borrowers.

The book data should be kept in a text file.

Your Tasks as a team:
Same as the tasks listed in Section 9.2.

Programming Challenge 9.4

The Tiny Airline needs an application to keep track of its flights.

A flight has a date, flight number, total seats, number of available seats, and the ticket price.

A manager can add a new flight and update the ticket price.

A customer can purchase tickets or refund tickets before the plane taking off. When a customer purchases a ticket, he or she should enter the date, flight number and number of tickets desired. The application should display the total price and deduct the number of available seats if it is more than the number requested. A ticket should be printed for the customer with the date, flight number, number of tickets for that flight, and total price on it. A customer can purchase more than one flight in one order.

A customer can refund the tickets through the help desk with the receipt. The help desk manager enters the flight number and number of seats returned. The number of available seats should be updated, and a new receipt is printed with the updated data.

The flight data should be kept in a text file.

Your Tasks as a team:

Same as the tasks listed in Section 9.2.

Programming Challenge 9.5

Tiny Bank needs an application to keep track of monthly statements for customers.

A monthly statement has an account number, customer name, statement beginning date, beginning balance, total deposit made, total withdrawal made, annual interest rate, and ending balance.

A customer can make a deposit, withdraw cash, and check the balance from his or her account. A deposit will increase the total deposit made, and a withdrawal will increase the total withdrawal made. Checking the balance will just display the ending balance.

A bank manager can search the monthly statement by customer account number and print one if found. A manager can also process the account, which will calculate the interest amount (annual interest rate divided by 12 and multiplied by the ending balance) and update the ending balance. After the balance update, the statement beginning date is updated to current date and time, beginning balance is replaced by the ending balance, total deposit made and total withdrawal made are reset to zero. A manager can change the annual interest rate at any time.

The monthly statement data should be kept in a text file.

Your Tasks as a team:

Same as the tasks listed in Section 9.2.

Programming Challenge 9.6

Update the Tiny Bank's application from Programming Challenge 9.5 so that each withdrawal and deposit amount and date and time of the transaction is kept for the account. These data are just for the current month. Once a statement is processed, the transaction history is cleared. The transaction history for the month should be included in the monthly statement.

The account data should be kept in a text file.

Your Tasks as a team:
Same as the tasks listed in Section 9.2.

9.16 Chapter Summary

In this chapter, you applied what you learned in the previous eight chapters in problem solving. You followed the process of building an inventory management system for Mr. Lincoln's toy retail store. You read how a team works on writing user stories, estimating stories and tasks, planning sprints, reviewing sprints, and team retrospective. You are encouraged to do similarly with the Programming Challenges provided in this chapter.

CPSIA information can be obtained
at www.ICGtesting.com
Printed in the USA
LVHW010320260822
726878LV00006B/462